CONTENTS

PREFACE AND SUMMARY

Unemployment rates in Canada have been rising almost continuously since the mid-1960s. This has been a matter of considerable concern to Canadians. The persistingly high rates of unemployment have been taken as a sign of fundamental failure in the Canadian economy.[1] The steady increase in the unemployment rate has been attributed to structural changes in the labour force and as the harbinger of the post-industrial society.[2]

The problem of unemployment has been the subject of a number of past Fraser Institute studies.[3] The present study, undertaken by Herbert Grubel of Simon Fraser University and Josef Bonnici of Deakin University, attempts to get an analytical handle on this crucial issue by focusing on the relationship between the unemployment situation in Canada and that in the United States. In particular, persistently high rates of unemployment in Canada are analyzed in the context of the divergence of Canadian/U.S. unemployment rates in more recent years.

In their analysis of the reasons for this divergence, Grubel and Bonnici do not find that the traditional Keynesian or macro-economic determinants of unemployment explain recent North American developments. Focusing on 1984, the last year for which full information is available, Grubel and

---

1. See Walter Block, *Focus: On Economics and the Canadian Bishops,* Vancouver: The Fraser Institute, 1984.

2. The economics of the structural change in the Canadian economy is the subject of an ongoing investigation at the Fraser Institute. Preliminary findings do not support the casual impression that the emergence of the "services economy" means an inevitably higher rate of unemployment.

3. *Unemployment Insurance: Global Evidence of Its Impact on Unemployment,* Ed. H.G. Grubel and M.A. Walker, Vancouver: The Fraser Institute, 1978. See also, *Focus: On Real Wage Unemployment,* D. Daly and D. MacCharles, Vancouver: The Fraser Institute, 1986.

Bonnici find that the net demand stimulation from imbalances in government spending and foreign trade netted out to zero in the United States but came to about 11 percent of GNP in Canada. In other words, the combination of government spending and trade developments should have added a net extra stimulus to the Canadian economy equal to about 11 percent of all the income generated in the country. This development should have caused the Canadian unemployment rate to be lower than that in the United States if aggregate demand developments were important. In the event, just the opposite situation has developed.

In analyzing monetary policy and its effects on the diversions of unemployment rates, Grubel and Bonnici find that monetary policy has had about equal effect on demand in the two countries.

Failing to find an explanation for the divergence of unemployment rates in the additional analysis of income and aggregate demand, Grubel and Bonnici turn to an analysis of the micro-economic aspects of the evolution of the two country's economies and here they discover some fascinating and very indicative results. For example, they discover that real wages in Canada have risen 40 percent faster than wages in the United States during the period 1965-1984. In their view this real-wage pressure has forced employers in Canada to use labour-saving capital and technology at a rate greater than U.S. employers. As a result, the productivity of those employed rose more rapidly in Canada than in the United States and real unit labour costs in the two countries have risen by about equal amounts. Unemployment has risen more because more labour was replaced by technology in Canada than in the United States and because of differences in institutions and government policies in the two countries.

Unionization rates which were at 30 percent in both countries in 1965 had gone to 40 percent in Canada and 18 percent in the United States by the early 1980s. The threat of unionization has made potential employers more reluctant in Canada than in the United States to hire the unemployed at lower wages in activities that undercut unionized firms. The consequence is to create an ''insider-outsider'' effect wherein members of unionized enterprises earn high wages corresponding to high rates of productivity but non-union members are frozen out of employment by the same process.[4]

---

4. The ''insider-outsider'' phenomenon has been identified in Europe and Scandinavia by the noted Swedish Economist, Assar Lindbeck (Lindbeck and Snower, 1985). Lindbeck is noted both for his past role as an adviser to the Social Democratic governments of Sweden and his role as Chairman of the Nobel Prize Committee.

In addition, the unemployment insurance systems of the two countries have diverged greatly. In 1970 the unemployment insurance systems in both countries had similar characteristics. The average benefit as a percentage of working income — the so-called replacement ratio — was roughly the same in Canada as it was in the U.S. Moreover, the total payment of benefits to unemployed persons represented an identical fraction of GNP in the two countries. By 1982, however, Canada's benefits percentage was twice as large meaning that the average worker received twice as large a fraction of his/her income when he/she became unemployed as was the case in the U.S. The result of this, in combination with more generous access provisions, was that the Canadian Unemployment Insurance system paid out 3.5 times more benefits than the United States.[5] The result is that the adjustment of Canada's labour markets to changing economic conditions is much slower than that in the U.S. because the penalty workers pay for selective job search and having high reservation wages is reduced by the unemployment insurance system.

Grubel and Bonnici's analysis strongly suggests that the solution to Canada's unemployment problem must lie in a realignment of real-wage and productivity levels. Their analysis suggests that closing the Canadian/U.S. unemployment rate gap requires a drop in Canadian real wages by between 5 and 13 percent. The results of such a drop would appear only gradually. The main policy recommendation is for institutional changes which raise the flexibility of real wages in Canada.

The Fraser Institute is pleased to publish the work of Herbert Grubel and Josef Bonnici in an effort to bring to Canada an element of discussion and public debate which, while widespread in Europe, has not yet been accepted in Canadian policy circles. However, owing to the fact that Grubel and Bonnici have independently arrived at their results, the views they express may not reflect severally or collectively the views of the members or the Trustees of the Fraser Institute.

Michael Walker
The Fraser Institute

---

5. For an analysis of the current status of the Unemployment Insurance System, see, M.A. Walker and D.G. Wills, "Unemployment Insurance, The Issues and the Options," *Fraser Forum*, Special Edition, 1986.

ABOUT THE AUTHORS

HERBERT G. GRUBEL

Since 1972 Herbert Grubel has been a Professor of Economics at Simon Fraser University. He was born in Germany and received his professional training in economics at Yale University (Ph.D. 1962). He held full-time teaching positions at Stanford University (to 1963), the University of Chicago (to 1966) and the Wharton School at the University of Pennsylvania (to 1971).

Temporary teaching took him to the University of Nairobi in Kenya, the University of Cape Town in South Africa and the Institute for World Economics in Kiel, Germany. Sabbatical and research positions were held at the Australian National University in Canberra, Nuffield College at Oxford in England, the U.S. Treasury Department in Washington and the Institute of Southeast Asian Studies in Singapore.

Professor Grubel has authored or edited 12 books and over 120 articles, many in collaboration with others. Most of his work has been in the general field of economics, but with some concentration in international trade and finance. His work has been supported by the Canada Council, the U.S. National Science Foundation, the International Monetary Fund and some U.N. agencies.

He is the author of four previous titles by the Fraser Institute and serves as a member of the Institute's Board of Editorial Advisers.

JOSEF BONNICI

Since 1980, Josef Bonnici has been a Lecturer at Deakin University in Geelong, Australia. He was born and raised in Malta. After four years of study in 1975 he earned his B.A. (Hons.) in Economics from the University of Malta.

Josef Bonnici came to Simon Fraser University in 1976, earned his M.A. in 1977 and his Ph.D. in Economics in 1980.

His dissertation and publication are in the field of dynamic input-output analysis for market economies. He teaches macro-economics and quantitative economics at Deakin University.

INTRODUCTION*

In this paper we develop the controversial thesis that Canada's high and rising unemployment rates in recent years have been caused by excessively high real wages and not by a deficiency of aggregate demand. In support of this view we consider Canada's unemployment rates in relation to those of the United States. As can be seen from Figure 1, the unemployment rates in the two countries have moved closely together and followed much the same trends between 1961 and 1985. However, while the gap in the rates of the two countries remained within a narrow range never exceeding one percentage point up to the mid-1970s, since then there have been two gaps with maximum differences of over two and four points. The growth of these differences represents an important puzzle, the explanation of which points to the causes of Canada's recent problems with persistent, high unemployment.

Our study uses very basic theories and time series, rather than sophisticated models and econometric techniques. We believe that our approach makes a persuasive case for the proposition that Keynesian demand management cannot explain the divergence of the two countries' unemployment rates and that the only other explanation is excessive wage rates. However, we accept the fact that only time will tell whether our analysis will hold up under more rigorous testing. In the meantime, many of the data assembled in this paper will surprise many Canadians, if we can go by the experiences we have had in presenting them to students and other audiences. If such surprise promotes further questions and analysis, the main purpose of this study will have been achieved.

---

* The authors acknowledge helpful comments received during seminars at the University of British Columbia, Simon Fraser University, the Universities of Konstanz, Frankfurt and Singapore. Special thanks for helpful comments go to Craig Riddell, John Chant, Steve Easton, Dennis Maki, Mike Walker, Shyam Kamath and John McCallum.

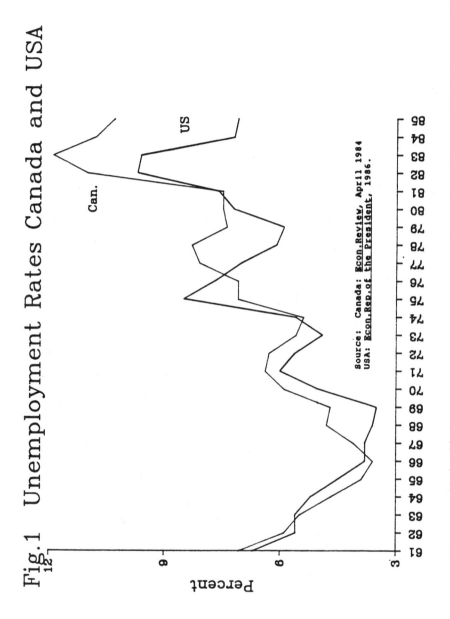

Fig.1 Unemployment Rates Canada and USA

Source: Canada: Econ.Review, April 1984
USA: Econ.Rep.of the President, 1986.

Before we begin the main parts of the paper, it is useful to put the topic and approach briefly into the following doctrinal perspective. Until the Keynesian revolution in economics, unemployment was considered to consist of frictional, structural, cyclical and real-wage components. During the post-war years the Keynesian revolution shifted the emphasis almost totally to demand deficiency as the cause of unemployment. During the last decade neo-classical ideas regained some currency under the labels of monetarism, supply-side economics, rational expectations and the new classical economics. In addition, many micro-economic models have been developed to explain how rational, maximizing behaviour by employees, employers and unions can be consistent with prolonged unemployment (see Lindbeck and Snower 1985).

These models have attracted much attention and empirical investigation in Europe. While the issue is far from settled, a growing consensus seems to be emerging that much of Europe's high unemployment since the early 1970s is due to excessively high wages (Grubb et al., 1983 and Malinvaud 1982). The OECD has accepted this diagnosis in recent annual *Employment Outlook* volumes. However, the question has received only little attention in Canada.

Helliwell (1983, 1984) considered real-wage and productivity developments in manufacturing in Canada and concluded that they cannot explain the growth in Canada's unemployment. A similar conclusion was reached by Ashenfelder and Card (1985). Our basic criticism of these studies is that they use econometric models and concepts that are deeply rooted in Keynesian approaches and which, therefore, have no room for the different ideas we present.

The analytical approach taken in this paper is likely to be rather new for most students of economics who have completed their university courses during the post-war years. During this period macro-economics developed as a new and self-contained course. Its aim was to explain that unemployment was due to insufficient demand. Other explanations of unemployment were omitted totally or given very cursory treatment. This is still true today.

One of the leading textbooks in economics in Canada (and through other editions in the world), is authored by the two celebrated Canadian authors, Richard Lipsey and Douglas Purvis, and the American, Peter Steiner. In its fifth Canadian edition published in 1985 about 95 percent of the entire material dealing with unemployment is occupied by the Keynesian theory of aggregate demand. Real-wage unemployment as an analytical class is discussed in about one page.

A final introductory remark is needed to prepare the reader for another way in which this paper is unconventional. Most Canadians now accept the idea that higher productivity and living standards can be attained only if employers are permitted to introduce modern, labour-saving technology.

According to the prevailing view, workers who lose their jobs as a result of the new technology will find employment elsewhere in the economy, just like others have for centuries of technological development. Our analysis does not challenge the validity of this view.

Instead, we consider the real-wage unemployment to be due to the introduction of too much labour-saving technology in the unionized sector of the Canadian economy. In other words, we will not present a modern version of the Luddite argument against technological progress, but rest our conclusions on the view that the absence of free labour markets has distorted the otherwise beneficial rate of capital formation.

Our introductory remarks suggest that the following analysis is quite outside the mainstream of conventional and academic economics in Canada. However, we have often been told by audiences with whom we discussed this study that our analysis is nothing but common sense and that it is accepted widely by people in the private sector.

I. THE ROLE OF DEMAND MANAGEMENT

During the post-war years, economists have emphasized demand conditions as the determinants of unemployment rates. This Keynesian analysis is well known. It postulates that aggregate demand determines national output (Y) and through it, unemployment. Demand consists of expenditures on consumption (C) and investment (I), government expenditures less taxes (G-T) and exports less imports (X-M). This model is recognized by many in the equation

$$Y = C + I + (G - T) + (X - M)$$

According to this model, national output and employment can be raised by expansionary monetary policy and the resultant lower interest rate. These encourage consumers and investors to increase expenditures. Demand can also be expanded through government deficits by either higher spending, lower taxes or both. The depreciation of the exchange rate also increases output by encouraging exports and discouraging imports.[1] Let us now com-

---

1. For a consistent interpretation of Canada's unemployment problems using this approach see McCallum (1984). Gordon (1985) noted that in North America labour economics has been traditionally a field separate from macro-economics,

- 4 -

pare Canadian and U.S. developments concerning these Keynesian determinants of unemployment by considering in turn monetary and fiscal policies and foreign trade.

Monetary policy

According to Keynesian theory the stimulative effect of monetary policy is measured by the market rate of interest. The close integration of U.S. and Canadian capital markets does not permit interest rates in the two countries to diverge significantly. This proposition is verified by the two top lines in Figure 2, which show long-term interest rates on Canadian and U.S. government bonds. Before 1983 the Canadian rate was above the U.S. rate by a small and rather constant margin. This margin is considered to have been due to the need of Canada to attract capital inflows. The narrowing of the interest rate gap since 1983 and the reversal of the relationship in 1984 suggest that monetary policy in Canada during these years has been relatively easier than U.S. policy as compared with earlier years. According to standard theory, therefore, it should have resulted in a narrowing, not a widening of the difference in the unemployment rates of the two countries after 1982.

In recent years, economists have paid increasing attention to real interest rates, which are nominal rates adjusted for expected inflation. If one considers actual inflation to reflect inflation expectations, then we may treat the difference between nominal interest and inflation rates as the appropriate index of monetary policy. The two bottom lines of Figure 2 show this index for Canada and the United States over the last twenty years. It can readily be seen from this chart that real interest rates generally have moved closely together. Exceptions to this pattern occurred during the period 1968-72, when the Vietnam War propelled U.S. inflation and brought down U.S. real interest rates. Similarly during the period 1979-80 the greater U.S. inflation following the second oil price shock brought negative real U.S. interest rates while Canada's remained positive.

However, most relevant for our purposes of analysis is the period since 1980, when the Canadian unemployment rates began to diverge so dramatically from those in the United States. In Figure 2 it can be seen

whereas in the United Kingdom and some continental countries it has always been an integral part of Keynesian economics. He believes this to be the reason why European economists and governments are much more aware than their North American colleagues of the problems of real-wage unemployement.

Fig.2 Longterm Interest Rates
(Gvt.Securities)

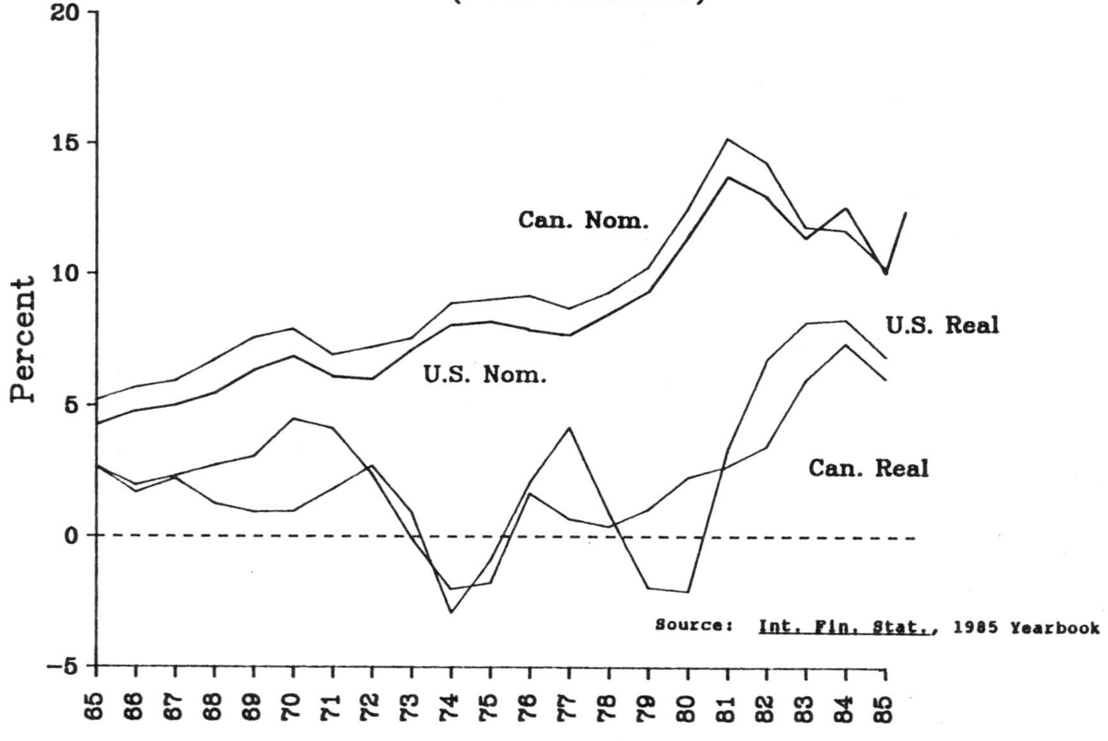

U.S. Real

Can. Real

Can. Nom.

U.S. Nom.

Source: Int. Fin. Stat., 1985 Yearbook

Percent

20
15
10
5
0
-5

65 66 67 68 69 70 71 72 73 74 75 76 77 78 79 80 81 82 83 84 85

that since 1981 real U.S. interest rates have been much above Canadian rates. By Keynesian analytical standards, therefore, the Canadian unemployment rates should have been lower than the U.S. rates. We can see that this has not been the case and conclude that for the period since 1981, the divergence in the two countries' unemployment rates is inconsistent with theories which stress monetary policy and either nominal or real interest rates as the primary determinants of unemployment rates.[2]

In a small open economy such as Canada's, the interpretation of monetary policy is complicated by international short-term capital flows and exchange rate changes. Basic theory in this context suggests that a country which pursues easier monetary policy than the rest of the world must accept a *depreciation* (not lower level) of its currency. During the period from 1976 through about 1985 the value of the Canadian dollar in relation to the U.S. dollar dropped by about 40 percent. This may be interpreted as indirect evidence augmenting that based on the behaviour of nominal and real interest rates. During this period Canada had an easier, but certainly not a tighter monetary policy than did the United States.

Fiscal policy

Figure 3 shows the deficits of the federal governments of Canada and the United States expressed as a percentage of GNP since 1965. The graph again reflects the close integration of the two economies generally. However, we note that since 1977 Canadian fiscal policy has been consistently more expansionary than in the U.S. Even the large Reagan tax cuts in 1980 have failed to make the U.S. deficits exceed those of Canada.

The data in Figure 3 do not tell the full story of deficit spending. In both countries total government sector deficits in recent years have been somewhat smaller than the federal deficits because of surpluses by social security systems and, in the United States, by state and local governments. The latter development is due to the fact that the majority of U.S. states had been forced to balance their budgets by constitutional requirements dur-

---

2. It goes beyond the scope of the present paper to examine the relevance of the theory for earlier periods, where we find some contradictory evidence. On the one hand, the low interest rates in Canada after 1972 had been associated with an almost uninterrupted rise in unemployment rates. On the other hand, the very low real interest rates in the United States between 1978 and 1980 did produce a sharp reduction in U.S. unemployment rates. For a discussion of Canadian post-war monetary policy see Grubel (1983).

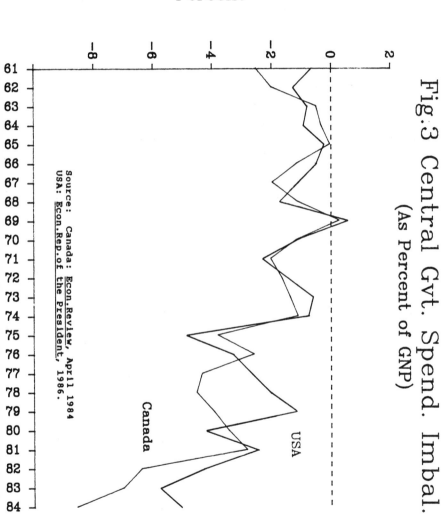

Fig.3 Central Gvt. Spend. Imbal.
(As Percent of GNP)

Percent

Source: Canada: Econ.Review, April 1984
USA: Econ.Rep.of the President, 1986.

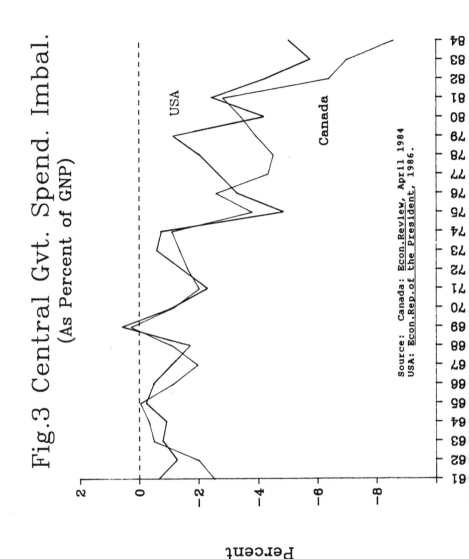

USA

Canada

Source: Canada: Econ.Review, April 1984
USA: Econ.Rep.of the President, 1986.

Percent

- 8 -

ing the 1980-81 recession. Since 1982 many of them have been running surpluses as the U.S. economic recovery caused revenues to rise more quickly than expenditures. In 1984 alone the combined surplus of state and local governments was estimated to have been $52 billion.[3] In total, in 1984 the total government sector deficits were 6.4 and 3.3 percent of GNP in Canada and the United States, respectively. This implies that in Canada other government sectors had surpluses equal to .6 percent of GNP while those in the United States were 1.5 percent of GNP (Wilson 1985, p.60).

Economists in Canada have made the argument that deficits since 1980 have not been large in a sense relevant for demand management policies because inflation caused a substantial reduction in the real value of the government's outstanding debt. Of course, this argument also applies to the U.S. deficit and therefore inflation rates in the two countries need to be compared. During 1981 and 1982 Canada had an inflation rate about 2.5 percent higher than the U.S. rate and the Canadian deficit therefore was somewhat less expansionary. However, during these two years the two countries' unemployment rate diverged very little. The really big gap in the rates has occurred since 1983, when the inflation and deficit rates were nearly identical. These considerations suggest that the adjustment for inflation does not alter the above conclusion.[4] The facts strongly support the view that differences in fiscal policy stimulus in the two countries are incapable of explaining, systematically, the observed differences in unemployment rates.[5]

---

3. There is, in addition, a significant difference in the actual cash requirements for financing the debt in the two countries. While the U.S. Social Security Trust Fund has been enjoying large surpluses which reduced the government's cash requirements, the Canada Pension Plan surpluses have been very small in comparison.

4. For a dissenting view on this conclusion see McCallum (1984) and Bossons and Dungan (1983), though it should be noted that these authors use only Canadian data and do not consider U.S. developments.

5. There exists a fairly widespread view that fiscal policy stimulus is measured inadequately by the quantity of deficit spending alone and that instead the analysis should also consider the *composition* of government spending. In this context the main difference in the U.S. and Canadian policies lies in high and increased U.S. military spending.

The widely publicized fact is that annual defence spending in the United States has doubled between 1980 and 1984 in nominal dollar terms. What is relevant for the present study of demand management is, however, what has happened

The foreign sector

In the above equation of demand, the last term referred to the foreign trade sector. The experience with this sector is presented in Figure 4, which plots the trade balances of the United States and Canada over the last twenty years, expressing them as a percentage of GNP. As can be seen, since 1977 the U.S. trade balance has been negative by a large margin. Since 1982 this imbalance has reached unprecedented magnitudes, attaining $120 billion or 3.5 percent of GNP in 1984. The Canadian trade balance, on the other hand, has been positive since 1976. In 1984 it represented about 4 percent of GNP.

In the Keynesian paradigm these figures imply that Canada has received a large positive stimulus to employment from the foreign trade sector, while the United States suffered a very large depressive effect. These developments clearly cannot explain the observed divergences in the two countries' unemployment rates. Instead, they add to the puzzle.

Summing up

Our analysis of monetary policy suggests that market forces have not permitted the development of large differences in nominal and real interest rates between the two countries and that the falling value of the Canadian dollar in recent years may be interpreted as a signal that Canadian monetary policy has been easier than that of the United States. The big difference in the two countries' Keynesian demand stimulation has come from the fiscal and foreign sectors. The U.S. federal budget deficits have been nearly completely offset by state and local surpluses and the foreign trade deficit in recent years. In Canada, on the other hand, the federal and provincial deficits and the foreign trade surplus all combined to stimulate aggregate demand. As a rough estimate, in 1984 they have added to purchasing power of the public a sum equal to about *12 percent* of GNP. For the United States this basic figure is near *zero*.

---

to this spending in real terms and in relation to the overall size of the U.S. economy. From this perspective, we note that U.S. defense spending as a percent of GNP was 5.3 in 1980, rose to a peak of 6.7 in 1983 and fell to 6.0 in 1984. These figures make it difficult to attribute much of the observed growth in the difference in the U.S. and Canadian unemployment rates to differences in the growth of defense expenditures.

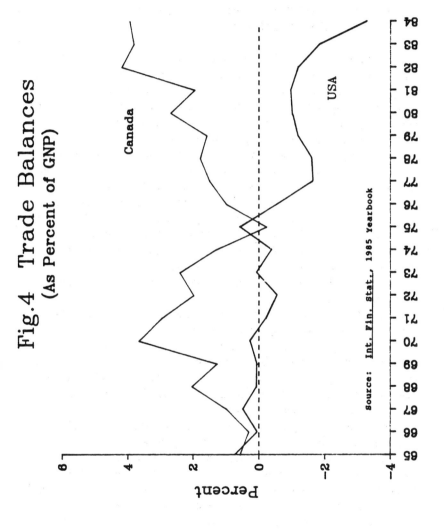

Fig.4 Trade Balances
(As Percent of GNP)

Source: Int. Fin. Stat., 1985 Yearbook

We believe that these data shed serious doubt on the usefulness of Keynesian theory in the explanation of the divergence of the U.S. and Canadian unemployment rates since the mid-1970s and most certainly since 1980.

II. THE NEO-CLASSICAL THEORY OF UNEMPLOYMENT AND MODERN EXTENSIONS

The neo-classical theory of real-wage unemployment is quite simple and represented by Figure 5, where the vertical axis measures real wages and the horizontal axis represents the quantity of labour either in a specific industry, an average for a representative industry or the entire economy. The labour supply curve slopes upward because labour force participation is an increasing function of real wages. Higher earnings induce many people with only marginal interest in employment to seek work. There is relatively little controversy over the proposition that the supply curve of labour slopes upward. The demand curve slopes downward for reasons which are central to this study and which, therefore, need to be analysed in some detail. To do so, it is easiest to assume that initially the economy is in full employment equilibrium. In Figure 5 this condition is shown to hold at point E where the wage rate is (w/p)0. Now let us consider that by some mechanism to be discussed further below, the real-wage rate in the country is raised to (w/p)1. Why does this change decrease the quantity of labour demanded from OQ0 to OQ2?

The quantity of labour demanded decreases because in the new equilibrium firms have substituted labour-saving machinery and equipment for labour, the relative price of which has risen. In the intermediate run the firms are induced to adopt labour-saving technology already available from their capital goods suppliers. In the longer run, the capital goods suppliers develop new technology appropriate for the new real-wage level and labour savings are even greater (Giersch and Wolter 1983).

More generally, the price elasticity of demand for labour is higher the longer is the time for adjustment to the higher wage rate. This time dependence of elasticities of demand and supply is universal, as OPEC, tin producers and other cartels have discovered in the recent past. For the purposes of the following empirical analysis it is important to note that, of course, this time dependence also operates and retards adjustment when real wages fall. Once excessively labour-saving capital per worker is in place, the capital intensity will be lowered only after the installed capital wears out. Investment in the development of excessively labour-saving

Fig.5 Labour Market Analytics

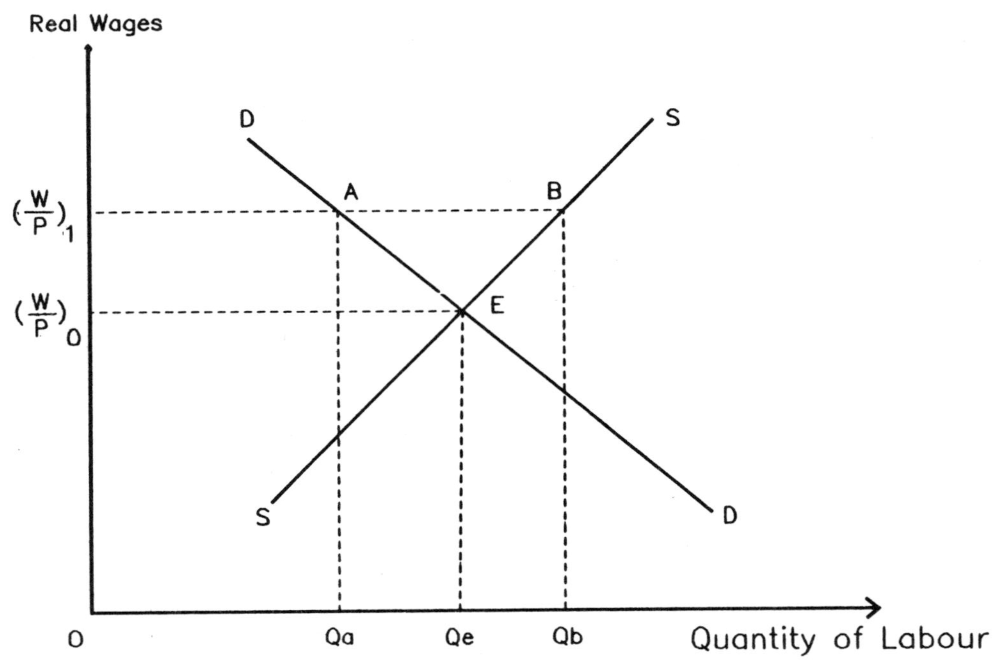

Real Wages

$(\frac{W}{P})_1$

$(\frac{W}{P})_0$

S

D

B

A

E

D

S

O   Qa   Qe   Qb

Quantity of Labour

technology in turn may never be abandoned if it saves both labour and capital in appropriate amounts.

We should notice an important characteristic of point B in Figure 5. Employers are on their demand curve for labour and they are in equilibrium in the sense that profits are providing the risk-adjusted rate of return needed to attract capital into the country. In this equilibrium the marginal productivity of labour is equal to the real wage received by the workers, just as it was at point E. In both situations *employed* workers fully earn their wages.

Statistics which trace the development of productivity and wages through time under these equilibrium conditions would show that real wages are not excessive in either situation. They indicate that wages and productivity have risen at the same rate. Yet it is clear from Figure 5 that the wage rate $(w/p)0$ implies full employment while the higher rate $(w/p)2$ results in unemployment equal to the distance Q1Q2. The OECD (1985, pages 34-36) publication presents the relationship between productivity and real-wage growth in different countries, but it is one of the first to point to the negative correlation between real-wage and employment growth in Europe even when real-wage and productivity gains are the same.

It may be worth noting that the preceding models are in sharp contrast with the Keynesian theory. In Keynesian models of unemployment the neoclassical adjustment mechanism fails because reductions in real wages simultaneously shift the demand curve for labour inward so that the excess supply of labour is maintained. Out of this diagnosis of the cause of persistent unemployment came the Keynesian prescription for the outward shift of the demand curve for labour through government policies of stimulating aggregate demand. In the preceding section we have discussed the inability of this approach to explain the difference in the development of the unemployment rates in Canada and the United States in recent years.

Extensions

One of the problems with the preceding theory of real-wage unemployment is that it does not explain how rational labour market participants get to the excessively high wages discussed above which we simply assumed to exist in order to demonstrate their implications for labour demand. Furthermore, the theory does not explain why unemployed workers do not apply downward pressures on wages and thus restore full employment equilibrium.

In recent years attempts have been made by economists to develop models which remedy these shortcomings of the real-wage unemployment theory. These models are complex and rich. They cannot be reviewed here in detail.

Instead, we draw liberally on them in the development of our own eclectic formulation, which we believe is most appropriate for conditions in Canada and the United States. We introduce our model as we try to answer a series of questions that would be asked by someone who wishes to understand the development and the persistence of the unemployment disequilibrium at (w/p)1 in Figure 5.

Wage contracts

How can wages get to excessively high levels? According to contract theory, it is costly to negotiate wage rates. Therefore, wage contracts are not renegotiated every few seconds in the light of the latest developments of prices, costs and demand, but cover periods of some length, such as one or more years. When the wage contracts are set, on average, they are neither excessively high nor excessively low. This is so because, on the one hand, employers know that they need to pay a certain amount to attract the quality and quantity of labour they require to get highest profits out of their business. On the other hand, employees and their union representatives know quite well what firms can afford to pay while they remain in business and adopt technologies that preserve desired levels of employment.

Within the contract theory, excessively high wages arise when output prices rise less or costs increase more than had been anticipated by the parties that drafted and ratified the contracts. For example, wages for forestry workers may have been raised considerably in a two-year contract in the expectation that the prices of lumber in the world would continue an upward trend of some preceding years. However, if these expectations are dashed and lumber prices fall, wage rates in the forestry industry will be too high during this contract period. As a result there is unemployment, not because unions exercised their power, but because of unforeseen and usually unforeseeable circumstances. Frequently such unforeseen developments are due to government policies, especially those which quickly restore price stability.

Contract theory explains not only how unemployment develops but also why it persists. It takes time for old contracts to mature and new ones to be drawn up in the light of the new realities and expectations. Riddell and Smith (1982) and Riddell (1983) have applied these ideas to the Canadian environment and suggested the need for a shortening and better staggering of contracts throughout the economy so that disequilibrium wages last for shorter times and affect only a smaller proportion of all workers in the economy at any given time. Grubel and Spindler (1983) have pointed out that bonus pay systems, which determine real wages in the light of actual developments, would make it possible to have real-wage flexibility while most of the benefits of longer-run contracts could be maintained.

Theories of union behaviour

Basic contract theory cannot predict how rapidly excessively high wages should be adjusted downward. This is clearly an empirical question. However, as we shall see in the next section, Canadian real wages have not fallen since 1981 in spite of very high unemployment rates. How can such a fact be explained? More specifically, in terms of contract theory, why don't competitive pressures always bring lower wages when new contracts are written?

To answer these questions it is necessary to take a closer look at the assumption about the behaviour of unions made above. This assumption was that unions would demand wages that assured the existence of the firm and jobs. But this is too simple an assumption since, as the neo-classical theory implies, wage rates influence the number of jobs available in every firm and industry. For this reason, unions face a trade-off between higher wages on the one hand and smaller jobs and membership numbers on the other.

Economists have developed elaborate theories to model the behaviour of unions within these constraints (McDonald and Solow 1981; Gylfason and Lindbeck 1984). In these models, as in all theory, conclusions follow from assumptions and anything is possible. Empirical work in this field has not led to definitive conclusions, though it is interesting that union-membership as a percentage of the labour force has dropped continuously during the last 20 years in the United States and has risen in Canada only as a result of the unionization of public sector workers (see Figure 9 and the discussion below for more on the level of unionization).

In the light of these facts we feel justified in advancing the hypothesis that unions care very little about the effects of their wage demands on employment levels in their industries, as long as they do not suffer from an absolute fall in work places and union membership. This is so because the loyalties of union leaders are to *current* members of the union, or the insiders, as Lindbeck and Snower (1985) have called them. High wages which reduce employment growth hurt only *potential* members, the outsiders who have no influence on elections and union policies. This kind of union behaviour leads to especially rapid increases in real wages when fast growth in demand and prices for the industry's output requires expansion of capacity. This capacity growth is then achieved by the more intensive use of labour-saving capital amounts and technology than would otherwise be the case, but which leaves, nevertheless, union membership at the old level or growing slowly at best.

But even when there is little or no economic growth, unions are reluctant to accept lower wages if by some error in forecasting their policies have resulted in unemployment among their members. This is so because this policy means that union leaders in effect have to ask the very large majority of members, say 85 percent, to take a cut in real wages to help the minority of 15 percent without work. Union leaders have great difficulties in selling such wage reductions to the majority. For the empirical analysis below it is important to note that this reluctance is likely to be higher when union members are sure that their unemployed brothers are reasonably well cared for by the social security net of the government.

The reluctance to make wage concessions is strengthened further still if unions can use political pressures on governments to provide protection from foreign competition and give subsidies or other assistance to industries suffering from such high wage unemployment. During the last 20 years the political responsiveness of government to such unions has been quite high, but especially so in Canada. This experience undoubtedly has reduced the willingness of unions to accept reductions in real wages that have been driven up by incorrect forecasts.

The threat of unionization

While the preceding analysis explained why it is rational for unions to obtain what are excessively high wages in the light of labour market conditions, we now need to address the following questions: Why do the unemployed not undercut the employed by accepting work at a lower rate? Why is there a failure of entrepreneurs to start new firms employing non-union, low wage workers to compete with the unionized high wage producers? Such action would result in, or at least threaten, higher unemployment for the insiders in the unionized industries. They would thus increase pressures on unions to accept lower wage rates. There are two answers to these questions.

The first is that if the unions are strong enough, they can prevent the development of competition to their unionized industries by threats of unionization or boycotts. This sort of threat can raise the cost of entry for entrepreneurs interested in hiring the unemployed at the lower wage rate to the point where it does not pay. In other words, insiders have the power to prevent outsiders from threatening their privileged position. Methods for carrying out this threat are well known among employers in British Columbia where the labour code is especially supportive of such action. For example, unions can create trouble for employers who buy inputs from non-unionized suppliers. As a result, at least one large non-unionized B.C. producer of electronic communications equipment has enjoyed great success selling abroad but has been unable to sell to large, heavily unionized local firms. As another example consider the fact that B.C. newspaper unions have the ability to prevent the printing of advertisements placed by firms that are engaged in labour disputes.[6]

But the threat of unionization affects not only the creation of new firms and the hiring of the unemployed. It also limits wage reductions among the employed in the non-union sector. Employers know that they face an increased probability of unionization if they create too wide a gap between the wages they pay and those that are earned by the unionized workers. It is, therefore, rational for them to avoid the long-run costs of potential unionization with its impact on average wages and all of the non-wage contract complications and costs by paying higher wages. These actions in turn reduce pressures on the unionized sector to lower wages, even when they are excessively high because of unexpected developments after the signing of wage contracts.

---

6. During the recession and high unemployment in the early 1980s unionized supermarket chains lost large market-shares to competition from new stores that operated with non-unionized labour. Kroger's, one of the largest supermarket chains in the United States was strongly affected by this trend and in 1984 asked its employees in Pittsburgh stores to accept a reduction in wages. When the union refused such a contract, Krogers closed all of its stores in Pittsburgh. Obviously, it was more profitable to accept the losses from the store closings than those that would have accompanied continued annual losses from operations. In other regions Kroger's obtained substantial wage concessions from its workers. (According to *Business Week*).

   In British Columbia, supermarket employees have extremely high wages, with a check-out clerk earning about $17 an hour. The unemployment rate in the province has recently stagnated around 13-15 percent. Yet, there has been no competitive threat to the established supermarkets from new firms using non-union labour and consequently there have been no reductions in the employee's wages, as there have in the United States. We have asked economists, politicians, business men and many people familiar with B.C. economic conditions why there has been this difference in the developments in the two regions. The answer we received most often was that the threat of unionization and of union action against successful new store ventures made the investment too risky.

Social welfare legislation

The second main reason why the unemployed do not undercut the employed is that social insurance programs reduce incentives to do so. Unemployed workers face a certain expectation of getting rehired or finding a job at a high pay. If the social insurance benefits and the probability of finding a high-paid position are high enough, it is rational to remain unemployed since the value of the expected income is greater than that to be had by accepting the lower paid job (Grubel and Walker 1978). This conclusion is more likely to be realized the higher are potential earnings from work in the underground economy and the larger is the tax rate on regular income relative to that on social insurance and underground economy income.

Another reason why the unemployed may not undercut the employed is due to minimum wage legislation. Minimum wages prevent employment of the young and untrained because their productivity often is less than that wage warrants since they have had little or no work-experience and training (Mincer 1976; West and McKee 1980). Minimum wage legislation thus prevents these workers from giving competition to unionized firms. Through this mechanism it reduces pressures for the reduction of excessive wage rates set in the unionized sector.

The preceding analysis of the process whereby high-wage unemployment is created and maintained is essentially static. We believe that as such it misses an important element of reality, which can result in a ratchet effect and an upward creep in the margin by which real wages are in excess of equilibrium. This missing element of reality is that when wage contracts turn out to have resulted in rates that are too low because of forecast errors, unions find it in their rational self-interest and they often succeed in obtaining upward revisions. As a result, even if there is symmetry in forecasting errors, there is a bias because low wages tend to be revised upward more quickly and fully than high wages are adjusted downward.

Summing up

In this section we have discussed modern theories which attempt to establish why unemployment in the neo-classical model is created and can persist, even though it represents a disequilibrium and market forces should prevent its development and lead to its elimination. These theories involve an extension of the neo-classical model into a world with uncertainty and transactions costs. They also consider worlds in which labour markets are imperfect due to the existence of unions and minimum wage legislation and there are distortions due to the existence of social insurance programs.

We have taken from these modern theories elements which we believe to be particularly relevant to the comparison of Canadian and U.S. unemployment in recent decades. These elements are the existence of long-term contracts and the tendency for them to produce wages that are too high in the light of failure of output prices to rise as anticipated; the interest of unions to preserve these excessive wages because they accrue to the majority of their members; the unwillingness of unemployed workers to undercut the unionized sector because social insurance benefits and the rehiring chances make it unprofitable; the lack of profitability in establishing new firms or hiring unemployed workers at the lower wage rates because of the threat of unionization.

In the end, all of the above analysis serves to reinforce the neo-classical idea that persistent unemployment is due to excessive real wages and the adoption of excessively labour-saving technologies. In the next section we therefore focus on the relative development of real wages in Canada and the United States as the main explanation for the divergence of the two countries' unemployment rates. But the modern theories point to the need to find developments which can explain why the real wages developed as differently as they did in the two countries. According to these theories, unionization levels and social insurance spending are prime candidates for such an explanation.

III. REAL-WAGE AND PRODUCTIVITY TRENDS

Figure 6a plots the indices of average weekly wages in Canada and the United States between 1961 and 1983. The indices are equal to 100 in 1965 and both have been expressed in real terms after appropriate deflation by the consumer price indices of the two countries. The time series were both set at 100 in 1965 in order to permit the analysis to abstract from the absolute income differences between the two countries and to focus on the differences which developed since the time when unemployment was low and nearly equal for a substantial number of years.

The data show that until 1966 real wages in the two countries rose at identical rates. Thereafter Canadian rates went on a steep climb unmatched by U.S. rates. The peak in Canadian rates was reached at 140 in 1977, after which point the rates dropped. Since 1979 they have stayed at 135. U.S. rates by contrast reached a peak of only 105 in 1972-73 and since then have drifted downward at an irregular rate to 95 in 1983. The most striking fact revealed by this graph is that between 1965 and 1983 Canada's average real wages have risen by about 40 percent more than those in the

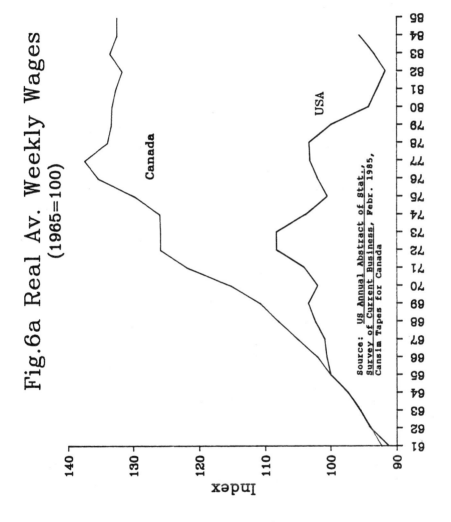

Fig.6a Real Av. Weekly Wages
(1965=100)

Canada

USA

Source: US Annual Abstract of Stat.,
Survey of Current Business, Febr. 1985,
Cansim Tapes for Canada

United States. In the light of the above theories it is evident that during this period there has been a much stronger incentive in Canada than the United States to substitute capital and technology for labour. Moreover, these facts are consistent with the development of the large gap in the unemployment rates between the two countries noted in Figure 1.

It is tempting to argue that the real-wage data in Figure 6a should be adjusted for changes in the value of the Canadian-U.S. dollar exchange rate. Such an adjustment is inappropriate for reasons which can be seen by considering the following thought experiment. Assume that initially Canadian and U.S. nominal and real wages are at 100. In the following period U.S. wages and prices remain unchanged but Canadian wages double along with a doubling of all prices. Under these conditions, deflation of the Canadian wages by the price index results in a real-wage index of 100 and the two countries' real-wage indices are the same, as events require that they should be.

Now consider the exchange rate. Under the postulated inflation in Canada it should double (or fall by one half, depending on the definition of the rate). If this new exchange rate were used to convert into U.S. dollars the Canadian real-wage index of 100, the result would show a fall of the Canadian real wage to one half of that in the United States. This result would clearly not be consistent with the postulated facts. We conclude that the comparison of real-wage rates of two countries through time requires the deflation of nominal wages by the respective country's consumer price index only. Further adjustment for exchange rate changes are not needed.

However, the preceding analysis needs to be amended by considering that in the longer run purchasing power parity holds and, *ceteris paribus*, there should be equi-proportionate changes in the exchange rate and differences in the two countries' inflation rates. If these conditions hold, it is a matter of indifference whether the nominal wages are deflated by the respective consumer price indices or whether they are compared by converting them into a common currency.

In the real world, of course, purchasing power parity does not hold at all times and there may be other influences on the exchange rate. Therefore, it is useful to consider the development of relative wage levels in the two countries using separately both the price indices and the exchange rate. For this purpose we constructed Figure 6b. It shows nominal average wage indices in both countries, but the Canadian data are converted to U.S. dollars. As can be seen, the information conveyed is much the same as in Figure 6a. Since the mid-1960s, Canadian wage rates have risen much more rapidly than U.S. wage rates. In the end year 1983 the percentage differences in wages is approximately the same. In Figure 6a the difference is about 40

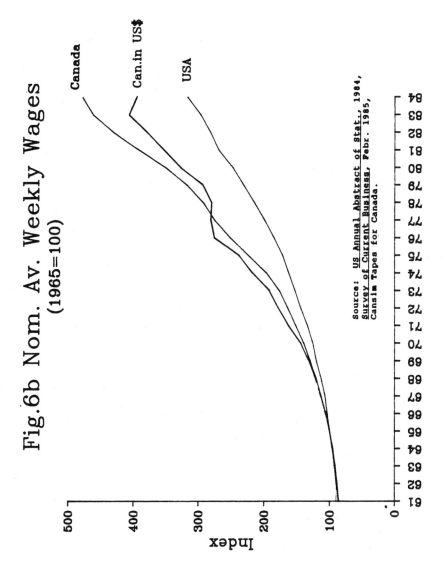

Fig.6b Nom. Av. Weekly Wages
(1965=100)

Canada

Can.in US$

USA

Index

500
400
300
200
100
0

61 62 63 64 65 66 67 68 69 70 71 72 73 74 75 76 77 78 79 80 81 82 83 84

Source: US Annual Abstract of Stat., 1984,
Survey of Current Business, Febr. 1985,
Cansim Tapes for Canada.

points, or about 43 percent on the base of 95. In Figure 6b the difference is about 110 points, which on the base of 290 is equal to about 38 percent.

Unit labour costs

In the traditional approach to the analysis of real wages and unemployment the preceding data are considered to be irrelevant since they fail to reflect changes in labour productivity in the two countries. To remedy this deficiency, in Figure 7a we present a time-series on real unit labour costs, which take proper account of changes in the productivity of labour in the two countries. The data were found in the original publication as they are shown except for the adjustment to the base of 100 in 1965 so that the analysis can focus on changes through time and abstract from the higher absolute level of income in the United States.

As can be seen, unit labour costs in the two countries moved together until 1974, when the Canadian costs went on a very steep climb from which they retreated at first quickly and then slowly to where in 1983 they were at the same level as in 1974. However, since U.S. costs fell continuously after 1974, in 1983 there was a gap of about 7 percentage points in favour of Canada. In Figure 7b the unit labour costs in the two countries are shown after they have been increased by the respective growth in consumer prices. According to this measure, Canadian costs are about 50 percentage points in excess of U.S. costs in 1983. When the Canadian series is converted to U.S. dollars, as is appropriate according to the above consideration, the gap shrinks to 8 percentage points, which converts to 3 percent on the U.S. base of 294.

The data in both Figures 7a and 7b suggest that Canadian wage rates are at an equilibrium level relative to those in the United States, since the observed differences in unit labour costs are negligibly small and may be considered to be virtually zero in the light of measurement errors which always beset statistics of this sort. This conclusion is supported by the evidence noted above, namely the strong competitiveness of Canadian industry in the U.S. market, which has led to the record export surpluses evidenced in Figure 4. According to the traditional approach to the analysis of unemployment, this result implies that the gap between the U.S. and Canadian unemployment rates in recent years is due to causes other than excessive real wages in Canada.

However, this conclusion is based on the traditional approach to the analysis of the effects of wage rates on employment, which we have criticized in the theoretical discussions above. This approach neglects the fact that the wage and productivity developments in these statistics concern only those

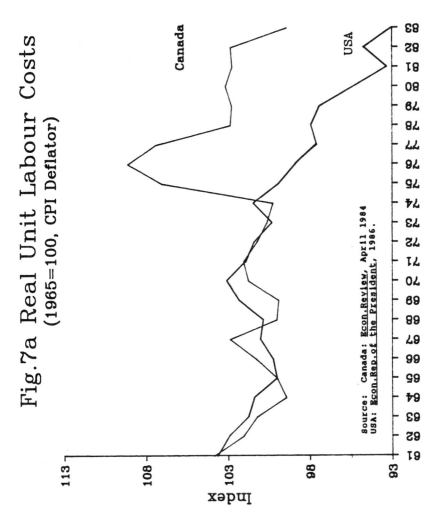

Fig.7a Real Unit Labour Costs
(1965=100, CPI Deflator)

Canada

USA

Source: Canada: Econ.Review, April 1984
USA: Econ.Rep.of the President, 1986.

Index

Fig.7b Nom. Unit Labour Costs

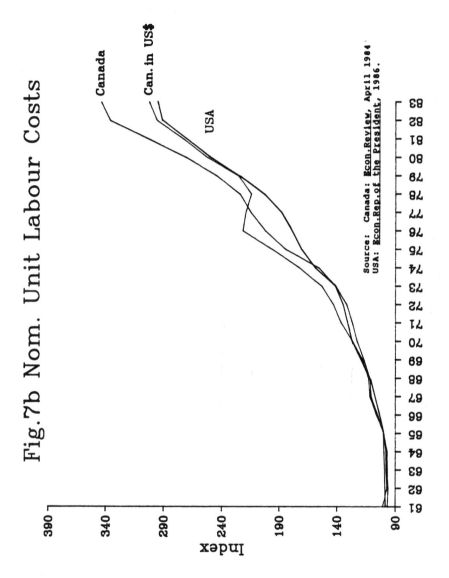

Canada

Can. in US$

USA

Source: Canada: Econ.Review, April 1984
USA: Econ.Rep.of the President, 1986.

workers who are employed. These workers have been bestowed with labour-saving capital and technology required to raise their productivity to the level needed to have them earn the high wages they are paid. But what has happened to those workers who have been made redundant by these wage and productivity developments? According to the new approach, they cannot find employment in their old industries because limitations of product and other factor markets make it impossible to expand capacity sufficiently. At the same time, these redundant workers are unwilling or unable to find employment at lower wage rates in other industries for reasons that were outlined above.

Figures 6a and 6b show clearly that since the late 1960s Canadian real-wage rates rose relative to those in the United States by ever larger margins. These labour cost differences induced Canadian employers to choose relatively more labour-saving technology than their U.S. competitors, starting from the 1965 base and given that both had access to capital at the same cost. For this reason we believe that the explanation of the difference in the two countries' unemployment rates is found in Figures 6a and 6b, which reflect the employers' stimulus for the adoption of a specific labour-saving technology, and not 7a and 7b, which reflect the longer-run response to this stimulus and which should show the result shown, whatever may be the wage costs confronting employers.

The timing problem

However, in support of our analysis we must now confront the fact that Canadian and U.S. real-wage rate growth began to diverge about 1967 while the unemployment gap developed only about ten years later and that the difference in the two countries' unemployment rate was zero in 1981.

We believe that the timing is explained quite simply by the boom and bust of the markets for natural resources after 1970. The global boom started in the late 1960s with expansionary monetary and fiscal policies in almost all industrial and developing countries of the world. These policies were adopted largely because of the widespread acceptance of the Keynesian model and the concept of the stable Phillips curve trade-off between inflation and unemployment. Accordingly it was believed widely that unemployment could be lowered permanently and significantly by the acceptance of some small and steady increases in inflation. The early 1970s also saw the Vietnam War as a major source of inflation and contributor to the natural resources boom.

Natural resource booms have important effects on Canada's economy. They improve her terms of trade and productivity in resource industries.

The growing demand for labour leads to shortages and bottlenecks. Under these conditions wages rise and it is rational to install labour-saving technology. For these reasons, the opening of the real-wage gap between Canada and the United States in the early 1970s was appropriate and did not lead to a divergence of the unemployment rates.

However, the boom of the 1970s was rather unique in history. It was accompanied by a major intellectual movement which created a widespread belief in pending ecological disasters, an exploding population bomb and the pending exhaustion of natural resources in the world. This movement was backed by the publication of the pseudo-scientific report of the Club of Rome and the 1974 OPEC oil price increases. During this period public opinion and attitudes in Canada came to accept the view that Canada's wealth had increased enormously since it was one of the main owners of natural resources and energy in a politically and militarily safe part of the world.

This was one of the main reasons why Canadian economic policy was made to diverge significantly from U.S. policy after the oil price shock in 1975-76. For the first time in the post-war era Canada did not deflate with the United States. Instead, the country geared up to meet the expected growth in demand for natural resources and energy. Expansionary monetary and fiscal policies were maintained in order to encourage real capital formation. At the same time, large wage increases were granted so that the new-found wealth would be shared equitably. In addition, high wages could be expected to increase the use of labour-saving technology, which was needed if Canada's small population was to be able to meet the expected world demand for natural resources. Wage and price controls were introduced to suppress inflationary pressures which were feared to result from the rapid wage increases. During 1975-76 the Canadian unemployment rate was below that of the United States, as can be seen in Figure 1.

However, the sharp U.S. recession during this period rapidly contributed to a fall in the demand for and prices of natural resources. As a result the Canadian unemployment rate rose in 1976 and 1977. The recovery of the U.S. economy after 1974 caused a significant drop in that country's unemployment rate and resulted in the first large gap in the two countries' rates. The recovery also brought a return to higher resource prices and demand, which is reflected in a small dip in Canada's unemployment rate. This growth in demand for natural resources was taken widely as evidence of the correctness of the predictions for global scarcities. It prompted the second OPEC oil price increase in 1979 and another sharp U.S. recession. The resultant rise in the U.S. unemployment rate caused it to be equal to that in Canada in 1979-80.

In 1980 the Reagan era began with tight monetary policy and a strong and convincing effort to break the inflationary expectations in the Western world. This effort was accompanied in 1981 and 1982 by the world's deepest recession and the highest unemployment rates in the post-war years. For Canada, the most important effect of these events has been the collapse of world prices and demand for natural resources. This collapse has lasted so long and has been so deep that the dominant expectations for global scarcities was replaced by the perception of a permanent glut and the inability of the Canadian economy to compete with low-cost producers of natural resources in the developing countries. In 1982 the unemployment rate in Canada reached the historic post-war high of 12 percent. In provinces heavily dependent on natural resources, such as British Columbia, it reached 15 percent.

In 1982 the U.S. government adopted a large tax reform and cut. This resulted in the longest economic recovery in the history of the country, a large appreciation of the exchange rate and sharp reductions in the unemployment rate. These developments brought also a reduction in Canada's record unemployment rates. However, as can be seen from Figure 1, the gap between the two countries' rates remained at its historic highs. According to the central thesis of this study, this gap did not disappear, as it had in the past, because the increased demand for natural resources stemming from the U.S. recovery was met by firms that produced their output with excessively labour-saving technology.

In sum, the preceding analysis attempted to explain the time-profile of the gap in the U.S. and Canadian unemployment rates by the fact that the expectations of global natural resource scarcities of the 1970s led to rapid wage increases to share the new-found wealth. The high wages induced the adoption of extensive labour-saving technology, which could have been used to produce large quantities of natural resources with the existing labour if the high demand for natural resources had materialized. The high wages and labour-saving technology were in fact appropriate for the boom years of the 1970s. However, during the periods of more normal demand for natural resources in 1976-78 and after 1982, the high wages and correspondingly labour-saving technology have resulted in the appearance of the large gap in the unemployment rates that is so striking in Figure 1.

Constant real wages

One of the most interesting facts revealed by Figure 6a is that between 1977 and 1983 average real wages in Canada have remained virtually constant. This constancy is very surprising since after 1980 unemployment rates in

Canada have been at record levels. In competitive labour markets such unemployment should create strong pressures for the downward adjustment of real-wage rates. Certainly, enough time has elapsed for the revision of most wage contracts, which should have come up for renewal during these years. The fact that these adjustments have not taken place must be interpreted as evidence in support of the model of union behaviour and impact developed above.

While it is true that during this period of high unemployment real wages did not continue the rise of the preceding decade, it is surprising that the depreciation of the exchange rate after 1976 did not lead to a lowering of the real wage. One of the most fundamental economic models of the international adjustment process stresses the fact that the depreciation of an exchange rate leads to rising prices in that country. In a competitive labour market environment the inflation accompanying currency depreciation tends to lower real wages even when nominal wages are fixed. It thus leads to a restoration of international competitiveness and, important for the present study, the adoption of the proper labour-using technology. The absence of this adjustment further supports the above propositions about the lack of competitiveness of the Canadian labour market.

A stylized description of the B.C. forest industry

It may be useful to illustrate the main points of the preceding analysis by describing some recent developments in the B.C. forest industry. It is well known that during most of the 1970s this industry enjoyed a substantial boom. Prices and output rose at rapid rates and the mood of the industry, employees, employers and responsible government agencies was one of great optimism. It was characterized by growing concern with future shortages of timber rather than shortages of demand or low prices.

Under these conditions the forestry workers' union, under the leadership of Jack Munro, was able to gain record-setting wage increases. Wage costs in the industry reached an average of about $22 an hour in 1982. At the same time, the union leadership realized that such wages could be paid only if labour productivity increased correspondingly. For this reason, the union agreed to let employers install the most labour-saving technology possible.

In 1981 and 1982 the U.S. recession and high interest rates created a slump in the B.C. forest industry as world prices and demand fell significantly. Such slumps have been usual in the industry, though this one was particularly severe. However, after 1982 output in the industry recovered, partly because of the growth in the U.S. economy and partly because of the depreciation of the Canadian dollar and lower interest rates generally. The lower dollar permitted the B.C. industry to make large gains in market share in the United States, which will long be remembered because of the actions against dumping which were taken by the U.S. industry. The remarkable aspect of this recovery is that it has not resulted in the usual return to full employment in the industry, even when in 1984-85 at times the physical volume of shipments reached higher levels than had been attained in the boom years of the 1970s. This fact is strong evidence in support of the main thesis of this study. The failure of employment to recover in the industry is due to the installation of labour-saving capital and technology. One large modern mill opened in Vancouver in 1985. It produces one-third more output while it uses half the number of workers than did the mill it replaced.

The neo-classical theory suggests that the high unemployment among forestry workers (about 25 percent in 1981-83 and around 15 percent since) should have led to the establishment of new firms which hire these workers at below union wage rates. There has been some development of this sort in British Columbia, but the threat of subsequent unionization of successful firms is so great that few workers have found employment in old and new non-unionized firms in the industry. One of the main effects of the high unemployment rate has been that some of the large forestry companies and other B.C. firms have turned increasingly to contracting out of certain operations that can be undertaken by small firms employing non-unionized workers. The small size of these firms provides reasonable protection from later unionization. However, the "problem" of contracting out is expected to be raised as a major issue by union negotiators in the next round of wage bargaining.

Also consistent with our model are the demands of the forestry worker unions for help from the government. One of these demands, which was granted in 1985, involved the administrative tightening of an existing ban on the export of unprocessed logs. This old law has the effect of raising the demand for saw-mill operators in British Columbia. In effect, it represents an increase in taxes on employers which are forced into undertaking an operation that otherwise they considered to be not profitable. This and other government policies have lowered pressures on employed forestry workers to accept reductions in real wages which would hasten the installation of appropriate capital and technology and thus the restoration of full employment in the industry.

The key correlation

Figure 8a contains four time-series which reflect a remarkable set of correlations. We believe that they provide some strong support of our hypothesis that at least since the mid-1970s Canada has suffered from neo-classical real-wage unemployment. The basic time-series shows the differences between the Canadian and U.S. unemployment rates. The others represent the differences between the U.S. and Canadian average real weekly wages in domestic currencies, nominal unit labour costs and real unit labour costs, all indexed so that the difference shows as zero in 1965. To permit easy visual comparisons, the difference in the unemployment rates was inflated by a factor of 10.

The real-wage theory of unemployment implies that the unemployment rate difference between the two countries should be an increasing function of the difference in the two labour costs between the two countries. The patterns of the time trends in Figure 8a lends strong support to the theory. As can be seen, between 1961 and 1974 the differences in the unemployment and the indices of wage rates and costs followed no systematic trend. However, after the growth in the real-wage and unit labour cost gaps in 1974, the unemployment rate gap commenced a similar climb.

However, most remarkable is the correlation between the nominal unit labour cost indices and unemployment rates of the two countries. For easier visual interpretation, Figure 8b shows only these two time-series. As can be seen, after 1974 there is an extremely close correlation between the two time-series. The unemployment rate gap changes almost exactly one year after the development of a gap in the nominal unit labour cost index. Rates of change as well as turning points coincide very closely.

In a sense this finding is a puzzle to us. Theoretically, the observed correlation of the unemployment gap should be with real unit labour costs. As Figure 8a shows, there is indeed a fairly strong correlation between the nominal unit labour cost series and the real unit cost series, on the one hand, and the unemployment series on the other. However, the correlation between the last two series is not nearly as strong as is the one between the series shown in Figure 8b.

In spite of the theoretical puzzle, we believe that the data in Figures 8a and 8b show a sufficiently strong correlation between differences in the indices of labour costs of production and unemployment rates in the two countries to serve as powerful evidence in support of our basic theory.

We have tested our theory somewhat more rigorously by the following econometric measurements. Using the Canadian unemployment rate as the dependent and the U.S. unemployment rate as the independent variable,

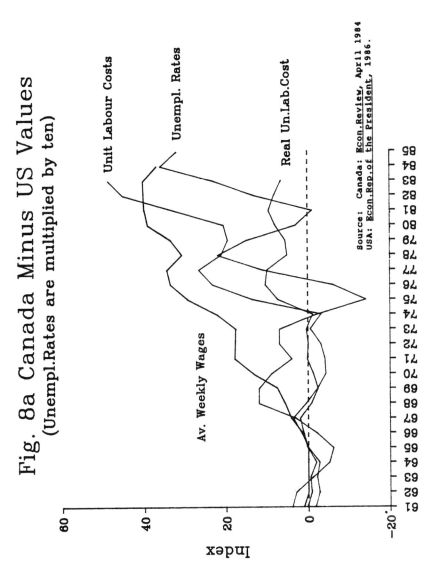

Fig. 8a Canada Minus US Values
(Unempl.Rates are multiplied by ten)

Unit Labour Costs

Unempl. Rates

Real Un.Lab.Cost

Av. Weekly Wages

Index

Source: Canada: Econ.Review, April 1984
USA: Econ.Rep.of the President, 1986.

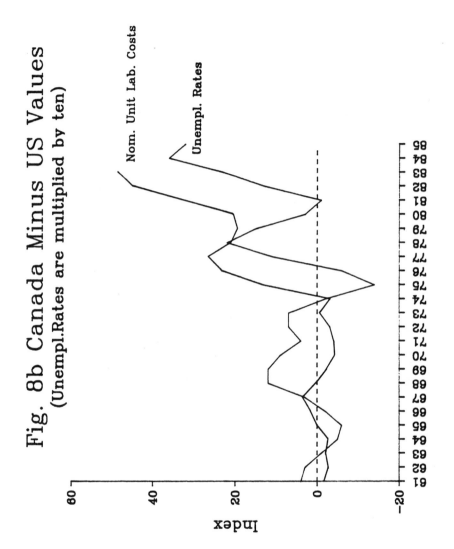

Fig. 8b Canada Minus US Values
(Unempl.Rates are multiplied by ten)

Nom. Unit Lab. Costs

Unempl. Rates

Index

we obtained a correlation coefficient or .75 (R-squared), as one would have expected given the close integration of the two countries' economies. We then added as an additional independent variable the difference in the two countries' real weekly earnings, as our theory suggested. The result was the following equation estimate:

$$URCA = .86 + .815 \; URUS + .044 \; DIF$$

where URCA is the Canadian and URUS is the U.S. unemployment rate and DIF is the difference in the real-wage rates of the two countries. The R-squared is .85 and the T-Values on the regression coefficients are 1.3, 6.0 and 2.8, respectively. The data covered 23 years and the time-series were adjusted for auto-correlation. The Durban-Watson statistic is 1.6.

Summing up

We believe that the empirical evidence on the development of real-wage costs in Canada and the United States since the early 1960s presented in the graphs is remarkably consistent with the neo-classical theory of real-wage unemployment developed in the preceding section. Especially striking is the correlation between the time-series on the differences of the two countries' real average wages and the unemployment rates. As expected, it is the development of domestic real-wage costs which determines the choice of labour-saving capital intensity and technology and which, therefore, determines the unemployment rate.

We need to reiterate here that the preceding analysis does not constitute an argument against technological innovation and labour-saving technology. These processes are needed for the attainment of higher productivity and economic growth. The preceding analysis argues that these processes were pushed to an inefficient excess in Canada during the 1970s. The push stemmed from organized labour and was granted by employers and governments in the expectation of permanent natural resource shortages and high prices in the world. However warranted these expectations may have been at the time, they were found to have been incorrect in the 1980s.

We should also note that the preceding analysis is consistent with the view that high union wages and appropriate labour-saving technology in some industries do not by themselves result in unemployment. If the workers replaced by the labour-saving technology accept low enough wages, they can always find employment. In this sense, the wage raising activities of unions cause differences in wages between the unionized and non-unionized sectors of the economy but not unemployment. However, this argument breaks down if threats by unions, minimum wage laws and generous social security payments prevent wages from falling to the appropriate levels in the non-unionized sector. Evidence on the constancy of average real wages in Canada during the 1980s suggests that wage rates in the non-union sector have been kept up when competition should have lowered them.

IV. SOME POSSIBLE OBJECTIONS TO THE CENTRAL THESIS

In Canada the view is widely held that the unemployment problems of the country in the 1980s are due to excessively low world demand and prices for natural resources. The proposition is supported by the fact that unemployment rates are particularly high in Canadian provinces which are dependent on natural resource production and that in the United States regions dependent on the same industries also have failed to share fully in the recent U.S. recovery.

These arguments are quite clearly correct and we have dealt with them to some extent in the preceding section. An increase in demand for and prices of natural resources would lead to increased profits and higher rates of return to investment by natural resource firms in Canada. All else remaining the same, these firms would expand capacity and even though they used the same labour-saving technology that we argued is inappropriate for the low product prices and demand, they would hire more labour and the unemployment rate would drop.

However, two things need to be noted about this scenario. First, for it to hold labour cannot insist on even higher wage rates as natural resource demand and prices increase. If the past is any guide to the future, we cannot count on such restraining behaviour by labour, though the very high unemployment rates of the 1980s may have encouraged a change in attitudes. Second, before we can use the insight about the role of low prices as a guide to policies, we need to assess the probability that natural resource prices will recover some time soon.

We have discussed this matter already in the context of the analysis of the timing of unemployment in the preceding section. In essence, we believe that the boom prices of the 1970s were the outcome of a global explosion of national money supplies which produced a temporary and unsustainable excess demand for all goods. This condition was reversed with the recession of 1980-81 and a global reduction in money supply growth rates. The end of the ability of OPEC to control the market and prices for oil in 1985 is symbolic of the end of the unusual conditions of the 1970s. There is instead now a high probability that the "low" prices of the 1980s are normal and that growing competitive supplies of natural resources from developing countries will for some time outstrip the growth in global demand. While there will undoubtedly be booms in the future, it is highly unlikely that we will soon see one strong enough to justify Canada's present level of real wages. Certainly, the Club of Rome predictions about pending global shortages should now be treated with the same scepticism as Malthus's predictions of a pending overpopulation of the earth have been treated for some time.

Demographic developments

It is logically possible that differences in population growth rates, age profiles and labour force participation rates between Canada and the United States are responsible for the observed divergences in the two countries' unemployment rates in recent years. According to this argument, the ability of any economy to create jobs is limited and, therefore, the greater the growth in the supply of people looking for jobs, the greater is the unemployment rate.

This argument does not invalidate the basic proposition of this study. As long as the demand curve for labour slopes downward the quantity of labour demanded is greater the lower is the wage rate. Therefore, for any given growth in the supply of labour, there is always one average wage rate at which there is no unemployment.

However, continuing in the spirit of this study, we have assembled data relevant to the issue of labour supply in the two countries. Figure 9 shows that Canada's population growth rates were above those of the United States in almost all of the 22 years under study, except in 1971, 1978-80 and 1984. The averages for the period were 1.39 and 1.11 percent for Canada and the United States, respectively.

We offer the following interpretation of the population time-series. First, in the 1960s when the Canadian was always and by a large margin above that of the United States, the differences in the unemployment rates were not consistent. This fact establishes a strong supposition that there is no necessary relationship between population growth and unemployment. Second, when next the Canadian rate exceeded the U.S. rate of population growth in the 1970s the Canadian economy was in the midst of the natural resources boom. It had produced labour shortages and led to accelerated immigration, which gave rise to the greater population growth rate. Clearly, the differences in the unemployment and population growth rates of the two countries were inversely related during these years.

Third, the first time that the Canadian unemployment rate was much above the U.S. rate in the late 1970s, the Canadian population growth rate was below that of the United States. In these years Canadian immigration was

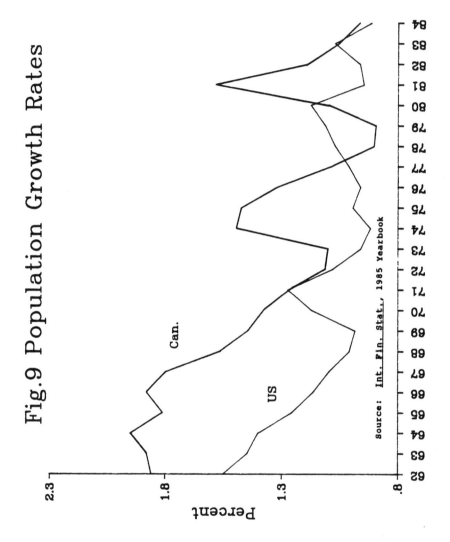

Fig.9 Population Growth Rates

Source: Int. Fin. Stat., 1985 Yearbook

cut back in the light of the recession in the country. The same could be said about the 1980s except that the 1981-82 figures were distorted by the immigration of large numbers of refugees from Southeast Asia. While these immigrants may have contributed to the observed differences in the two countries' unemployment rates, the differences in the population growth rates are so small that they are incapable of explaining a significant part of the gap in the unemployment rate.

However, raw population growth data fail to deal with the fact that certain age groups have different propensities to be out of work. In fact, S. Kaliski (1984) has argued that Canada's high unemployment rates in recent years have been due to an unusual age structure of the work-force. Thus, the population in the age-group 15-24, the baby-boomers of the 1950s and early 1960s, represent an uncommonly large proportion of the total labour force. Since they are more likely to be unemployed than older workers, for a variety of reasons that need not concern us here, they account for a substantial part of the increased unemployment rates during the 1970s and in recent years. The optimistic forecast of this analysis is that with the pending maturing of the baby-boom generation, Canada's unemployment rate will soon start to decline automatically.

There is no doubt that Kaliski's analysis and calculations are correct, but they need to be seen in the light of developments in the United States if we wish to explain differences in the two countries' unemployment rates. For this purpose we have calculated the percentage which the population aged 20-24 represented of the total population aged 15 and over for Canada and 16 and over for the United States. In 1975, the figure was 12 for the United States and 11 for Canada. In 1975, 1980 and 1983 the statistic was the same 12 percent for both countries. We conclude, therefore, that the age-structure argument cannot explain the divergence of the unemployment rates between the two countries since the mid-1970s.[7]

Finally, we need to examine the possibility that differences in the two countries' labour force participation rates are capable of explaining the gap in the unemployment rates. Again, this issue has to be addressed at the theoretical and empirical level. Theoretically, labour force participation rates

---

7. There has been a substantial difference in labour force participation rates in Canada and the United States. Resource constraints prevent us from pursuing this topic here. However, it should be noted that participation rates are endogenous to the level of wages. In addition, in the next section we present some data which explain the recently developed differences in the real-wage flexibility of the two countries' labour markets. Participation rates are also likely to be endogenous to these.

are at least partly endogenous to wage rates. In terms of Figure 5, the upward slope of the labour supply curve is due largely to an increase in the participation rate. Therefore, an excess of Canadian over U.S. labour force participation rates would be perfectly consistent with the gap in the unemployment rate which we are trying to explain.

However, the data show that U.S. labour force participation rates have been consistently above Canadian rates, as we might expect, given that the absolute level of wages in the United States has been historically above that in Canada. In 1970 participation rates were 64.5 and 66.8 and in 1984 they were 72.8 and 73.4 for Canada and the United States, respectively (OECD 1985, p.37). Similar differences existed in intervening years, though there appears to have been a slight narrowing in the gap through time, which again would be consistent with the slight narrowing in the differences in the two countries' wage levels during the period. However, we may conclude safely that labour force participation rates offer little explanation of the observed differences in the two countries' unemployment rates.

V. DIFFERENCES IN THE DETERMINATION OF WAGE FLEXIBILITY

The preceding analysis raises the important question why real-wage rates in Canada have been so different from those in the United States since about 1970. In the following, we offer as possible explanations of the differences between the two countries the existence of four institutional characteristics and policies.

Unionization

Figure 10 plots the levels of unionization of the labour forces in Canada and the United States since 1960. As can be seen, since 1964 the levels in the two countries have diverged continuously. The U.S. rate has dropped to a low of about 20 percent in 1983, while the Canadian rate has risen to 40 percent in the same year.

Unionization has many effects on the economy. It raises wages of union members by an average of about 15-30 percent above those in non-unionized industries (see MacDonald, 1983). However, for the present purposes of analysis the most important effect of unionization is on the reduction of downward flexibility of wages described above. As we have argued, it is not in the interest of the vast majority of union members to accept lower wages to benefit the small and often unknown minority of the unemployed.

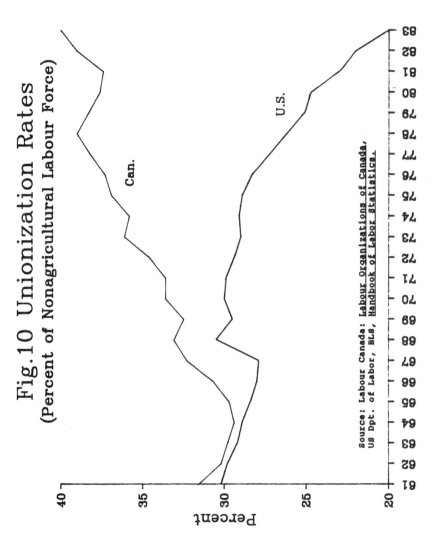

Fig.10 Unionization Rates
(Percent of Nonagricultural Labour Force)

Can.

U.S.

Source: Labour Canada: Labour Organizations of Canada,
US Dpt. of Labor, BLS, Handbook of Labor Statistics.

The rigidity of Canadian real average weekly wages after 1978 seen in Figure 6a stands in defense of this proposition.

It is worth repeating here that our model of union behaviour and real-wage rigidities does not mean that there should be a close correlation between unionization rates and unemployment rates through time such that whenever unionization rises unemployment goes up. Instead, the effect is more indirect. Whenever unforeseen circumstances, such as a reversal of world inflation and demand for natural resources, cause real wages to be excessively high, the rate of wage adjustment is slowed down by unions and the contracts they generate. It is for this reason that the strong reduction in world inflation in the early 1980s had such a different impact on real wages and unemployment in Canada and the United States.

Added U.S.-Canada differences

However, there are added differences between the two countries. Canada has a larger proportion of its work-force in natural resource industries, where economic rents represent particularly promising targets of union activities.[8] Canada also has a larger proportion of its output in regulated and government-owned or -operated industries. Unionization in the public sector is much more prevalent in Canada than the United States.

Unions in these government or quasi-government industries are especially effective in raising and maintaining real wages because their employers have no "bottom line" by which to measure efficiency and the use of appropriate

---

8. In British Columbia the government uses a system of stumpage fees to extract the economic rent from the province's vast forests. A report by the Economic Council of Canada pointed out that the system, in effect, leaves the rent as a residual after costs. Therefore, for a long time, forestry companies were willing and able to give in to union wage demands in the knowledge that they would not fall on profits but on government revenue. However, in the early 1980s wages had risen so much and the world prices of lumber products had fallen so much that revenues barely covered costs and many firms were forced to close operations altogether. The B.C. rent extraction system has been at the centre of U.S. attempts to establish that Canadian timber production is subsidized by the government. In comparison with the U.S. system of auctioning off the standing timber, the B.C. system involves what one might call a subsidy. But it has not gone to producers and is not available for export subsidization. Instead, it has gone to workers through extremely high wages and produced the province's record levels of persistent unemployment because the high wages induced employers to install excessively labour-saving capital and technology.

pay scales. For politicians it is much easier, within reason, to pass on higher wage costs through increased taxes than it is to accept strikes that create inconveniences for the public. During periods of overshooting in real wages due to changes in the inflationary environment, private sector unions lose members through unemployment and they get pressures to make wage concessions. These pressures are absent from unions in non-profit industries.

Regulation

It is now widely accepted that government regulatory processes which are ostensibly aimed at serving consumers, very frequently are captured by interest groups that make them serve their own ends. Especially the regulation of so-called natural monopolies like the airlines, buses, trucking and telecommunications has invited such capture (Stigler, 1971). The rate setting process for these public monopolies involves passing on higher real-wage and production costs to consumers, while adequate profits are assured for owners at the same time. Real wages in these industries, therefore, are not subject to competitive pressures and can remain constant or rising when unemployment is high and inflationary regimes have changed. Deregulation creates competition and real-wage flexibility. In the United States the deregulation of the transportation and communications industries began during the late 1970s and gained momentum in the early 1980s. The effects of this process on real wages have been especially dramatic in the airlines industry. Newly created airlines began to operate without unionized labour. They competed with the established monopolies, which lost money. In some instances regulated firms were forced into bankruptcy and emerged as union-free new enterprises. Many unions saw the handwriting on the wall and made wage concessions. As a result, average compensation in the U.S. airline industry has dropped substantially. Similar, though less dramatic changes have taken place in trucking, the bus industry and telecommunications in the United States.

In general, the effects of deregulation on union power and wage rates are likely to exceed those directly noticeable in these industries. We would expect that there are at least some psychological effects, from competitive battles between unionized and non-unionized firms in highly publicized circumstances as those which have involved U.S. airlines and buses.

In these industries employers ended up with wage and productivity concessions that were unthinkable before. Such outcomes must have put at least some damper on wage demands and the willingness of employers to grant them. At the same time, they should have strengthened the resolve of at least some workers and employers to resist the efforts of organized labour to unionize their firms. In Canada the deregulation of the above mentioned industries has been much less complete than in the United States. Therefore, there have been no corresponding reductions in real wages in these industries nor psychological effects on others. It should also be noted that in Canada regulation has been more widespread than in the United States even before the recent U.S. changes. Agricultural marketing boards in Canada, for example, have very strong supply management and therefore price setting powers. In the field of energy, government involvement has made prices and therefore wages less subject to world competition. As a result, during the drop in energy prices since 1981, workers in these industries have faced fewer downward pressures on wages than they would have in the absence of the energy policy.

It is obvious from the preceding analysis that the different experiences with deregulation in Canada and the United States in recent years can explain at least some of the observed differences in the real-wage flexibility in the two countries.

Social insurance spending

It is now widely accepted that social insurance programs of all sorts, but especially unemployment insurance, have the effects of raising unemployment rates.[9] That this is so can be seen readily by considering a person who earns $10 an hour or $400 a week which, after taxes and work-related expenses comes to $320, or $8 per hour. Such a worker in Canada receives unemployment insurance benefits equal to about 70 percent of *gross* earnings, which in the above example comes to $7 an hour and $280 for a 40 hour week. Abstracting from tax obligations on these benefits, the figures imply that the loss of income due to unemployment is $40 a week or $1 per hour. In other words, the cost of not working is reduced by the unemployment insurance scheme from $8 to $1 an hour, or from $320 to $280 a week. Under these conditions, it is not surprising that researchers have found the unemployment rate in Canada to have been an increasing function of the level of unemployment insurance benefits relative to earnings.

The relatively recent introduction of taxes on benefits reduce the disincentive effects of the system. However, the magnitude of this influence is an empirical question which can only be settled after it has been in operation

---

9. See Grubel and Walker (1978) for a detailed analysis of how unemployment insurance raises the rate of unemployment. It increases not only job-search but also seasonal employment, part-time work and strike-related unemployment.

for some time. We would not expect it to be very large on low income earners who face zero or low marginal tax rates.

Most important for the present purposes of analysis is the fact that these insurance benefits also affect wage flexibility. In the presence of such insurance-created low costs of not working, workers can afford to hold out longer before they accept employment at lower wages. This is the reason why we find so often that low paying jobs go unfilled even though unemployment is high. The high benefits also contribute to the reluctance of unions to accept lower wages for the benefit of the unemployed. At the same time, the benefits reduce pressures on unemployed workers to join non-unionized firms that undercut unionized competitors.

Canadian and U.S. insurance rates

Let us now turn to an examination of differences in the unemployment insurance systems in Canada and the United States. The left side of Figure 11 shows the generosity of unemployment insurance programs as measured by the percentage of work income which is replaced by benefits. The data have been taken from Grubel and Walker (1978) and OECD (1985).[10] The bar charts show that in 1970 the U.S. income replacement ratio was about 10 percentage points or 25 percent higher than that in Canada. However, in 1982 the Canadian replacement ratio was about 35 percentage points or nearly 85 percent above that in the United States. This fact by itself goes a long way towards explaining the greater Canadian wage rate rigidities noted above.

However, income replacement ratios are an imperfect index of the influence of unemployment insurance programs on real-wage rigidity and unemployment levels. Also relevant is the ease with which eligibility can be established, the maximum duration of benefits, the toughness with which administrators insist on evidence of job-search activity, the degree of coverage of industries, such as fishermen and of special conditions, such as pregnancy leaves. In all these and other dimensions, U.S. and Canadian unemployment insurance programs differ.

---

10. See *The Economist* (1984) which publishes the OECD figures found in this paper. They were taken from the 1984 *Outlook* volume. The data took into account not only the maximum replacement ratios under the law but also such other influences as the loss of other welfare and social service benefits accompanying the return to work.

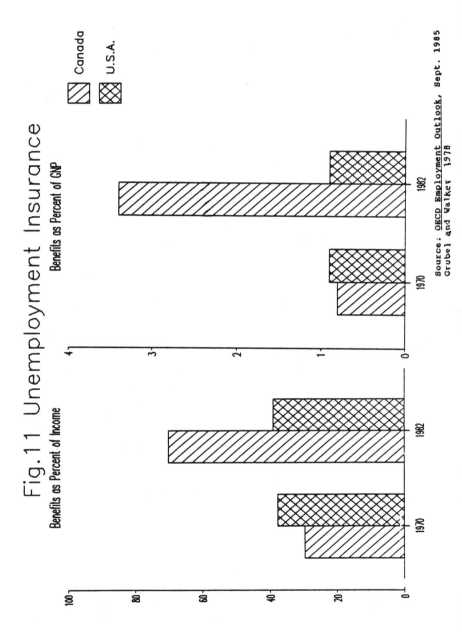

Fig.11 Unemployment Insurance

Benefits as Percent of Income

Benefits as Percent of GNP

Canada

U.S.A.

Source: OECD Employment Outlook, Sept. 1985
Grubel and Walker 1978

- 46 -

Fortunately, there exists a simple index that reflects the economic impact of these differences between the two countries' programs. It is shown in the right part of Figure 11. There we can see that in 1970, when the Canadian and U.S. unemployment rates were 5.9 and 5.0 percent respectively, the two countries spent roughly the same proportion, about .9 percent of GNP, on unemployment insurance benefits. After the pervasive liberalization of the Canadian program in the early 1970s, the spending data for 1982 are dramatically different. With the unemployment rates at 11.0 and 9.7, spending was 3.4 and .9 percent of GNP in Canada and the United States, respectively. The above arguments about the way in which unemployment insurance benefits impede wage flexibility are applicable also to other social insurance programs which make payment conditional upon the inability to work. Examples of such programs are accident and health insurance, social assistance to single mothers, Indians and other groups and the payment of subsidies to renters. In 1981, both Canada and the United States paid roughly similar percentages of GNP through such programs. Since then, however, President Reagan has attempted to get such payments reduced or at least to have their rate of growth slowed down. While he has not been very successful in these efforts, his announced intentions and the accompanying publicity is likely to have had important announcement effects with corresponding influences on the flexibility of wages. By contrast, the intention of Canadian governments not to reduce such benefit levels has been a major component of recent election platforms.[11]

Immigration policies

In recent years, Canadian immigration policies have been designed increasingly to "fine-tune" labour market conditions. This became apparent above in the analysis of population growth rates. Immigration rates were high during the low unemployment periods of the 1960s and 1970s and were low during the recessions, the biggest exception having been caused by the program for the admission of refugees in 1981-82. Perhaps more important, since the mid-1970s the proportion of all immigrants who were skilled workers decreased greatly at the expense of immigrants admitted on humanitarian grounds.

---

11. The public and government attitudes on this subject may be symbolized by conditions in British Columbia, where the widely publicized 1983 restraint program cut government employment and spending on highways and education. However, it raised the budget of the Ministry of Human Resources (Welfare) by 10 percent.

In the United States, on the other hand, immigration policies have been based on national origin quotas, which are insensitive to labour market conditions. It is also a well known, though poorly documented, fact that illegal immigration is much greater in the United States than in Canada. Immigration has a potentially important influence on wage flexibility since immigrants are known to be willing to accept wages at rates below those acceptable to long-term citizens. This is an ever present threat to workers and puts dampers on their wage demands. To the extent that this view is correct, the difference in Canadian and U.S. immigration policies and levels contributes to the explanations of the different wage flexibility in the two countries.

VI. SUMMARY AND POLICY IMPLICATIONS

In this study, we have examined the puzzling phenomenon of the growing and significant divergence of Canadian and U.S. unemployment rates since the mid-1970s. This divergence has reached a historically unprecedented 4 percentage points in 1984-85. The phenomenon is a puzzle in the context of Keynesian economics because during the last decade, but especially since the early 1980s, a comparison of demand stimulation from net federal and state-provincial deficits, the foreign trade sector and monetary policy suggest that Canada should have a much more buoyant economy than the United States. This has obviously not been the case.

To explain the puzzle we have introduced the neo-classical economic proposition that persistent, high unemployment rates are due to wages above their equilibrium. An examination of real-wage rate developments in Canada and the United States between 1960 and 1983 show that Canadian rates have grown about 40 percent more than those in the United States. These figures support the excessive real-wage argument as an explanation of the increased gap in the two countries' unemployment rates.

We found that unit labour costs in Canada have dropped in recent years sufficiently to restore the competitiveness of Canadian labour in the U.S. market. However, this fact is perfectly consistent with our central proposition that real wages are too high. Unit labour costs and competitiveness measures concern those who are employed and whose high wages have led to the introduction of the excessively labour-saving technology. We also discussed at length the question of why workers replaced by the high wages do not find employment at much reduced wages. We concluded that the threat of unionization and the generosity of social insurance programs reduce the opportunity and need for the lowering of wages and the creation of jobs in this sector. We have introduced empirical information to back our theoretical analysis and explain why Canadian and U.S. wage rate developments were so different. This information reveals that during the last 20 years some basic institutions in Canada and the United States have developed along very different lines, all of which are relevant to an explanation of the differences in the unemployment rates in the two countries.

The alternative to doing nothing

If our analysis and evidence are correct and there exists significant unemployment in Canada that is due to excessive real wages, the question then follows, what should be done about it. The most obvious answer is that real wages in Canada should be lowered. Clearly, this will be a very unpopular policy, difficult to advocate by any politician and, as we shall see below, even more difficult to put into place.

However, it has been suggested to us that it might not be desirable or necessary to lower wages at all. The alternative is to keep the high wages (and productivity) for those who are employed and look after the unemployed through the social security net. This policy would be superior to lower wages for all if the productivity of those working were high enough to permit the compensation of the unemployed and leave more income for those working than under the low wage needed for full employment.

We are not sympathetic with this viewpoint since we do not believe it to be true empirically. In addition, it neglects the great non-economic costs of unemployment, especially among the young who may ultimately be tempted to use non-political means to change a system that has so blatantly excluded them from the ability to live normal lives. It also disregards the disincentive effects operating on those workers and investors who are required to pay taxes needed to finance the social security net. Finally, we should point to the fact that there has been a fairly constant upward trend in the unemployment rates in Canada since the mid-1960s. After every short-lived reduction, there has been an upward surge from a higher base. This upward trend in the unemployment rate in our view is due to the excessive growth of real wages through time, which has been made possible by the growing strength of unions and the influence of growing social insurance spending and the other influences noted above. If there are no fundamental changes in any of these policies, there is every reason to believe that the upward trend of the unemployment rates will continue. In our view, the results of such developments are not desirable.

How much wage reduction is needed?

Let us now assume that it is considered desirable to adopt policies that lead to a reduction in real wages and unemployment in Canada. The first question that arises in this perspective is, by how much do the rates have to fall to restore full employment? The answer to this question depends on the debatable definition of full employment — a debate which we wish to avoid here. However, some empirical studies exist on the long-run elasticity of substitution between capital and labour, which permit us to provide some useful estimates of the amount of real-wage reductions needed to create equality between the Canadian and U.S. unemployment rates.

Hamermesh (1985) reviewed more than twenty econometric studies of these elasticities. He concluded that they are in the range of -.2 and -.5, assuming that wage changes have no macro-economic effects and firms' output is unchanged. An official study by H.M. Treasury (1985) of U.K. econometric evidence concluded that by considering induced output changes together with capital-labour substitution, the elasticities are between -.5 and -1.0.

An application of these estimates to conditions in Canada suggests the following. If the elasticity of employment with respect to real wages is assumed to be -.3 (the middle of the Hamermesh range), then it is necessary to lower Canadian real wages by 13 percent if employment is to be raised by 4 percent and thus made to equal the U.S. rate. If the elasticity is -.75 (midpoint of the U.K. Treasury estimates), then the same result is achieved through a lowering of the Canadian real-wage rate by 5.3 percent.

However, the preceding calculation is likely to involve an overestimate of the real-wage adjustment needed since it neglects the contribution of labour supply to the unemployment rate. As can be seen in Figure 5, if the supply curve of labour slopes upward, any reduction in real wages reduces the quantity of labour offered. Not much is known about the elasticity of the labour supply function. However, if we assume it to be the same as that of the demand curve, then the reductions in real wages needed to restore any desired level of unemployment is cut in half.

Unfortunately, the preceding empirical estimates of the cuts in real wages needed to restore full employment in Canada are rough and have to remain so. Much about the estimates of elasticities depends on the time horizon over which they are made. In the long run involving enough time for capital equipment to wear out and technology to adapt, elasticities may be even higher than the estimates cited by Hamermesh. But the time lags between the introduction of lower wages and the increases in demand for labour add further the degree of political risk involved in the policy approach.

How to cut the wage rates

Let us assume now that it is considered to be in the interest of all Canadians in the longer run that wages be reduced by the amount required to reestablish full employment. The big problem then is that in Canada's decentralized wage setting system the government has no direct and reliable influence on the level of wages. The federal and provincial governments can limit wage increases in the public sector, which include education and all of the Crown corporations. However, for the rest of the economy, influence can only be exercised through direct wage and price controls and macroeconomic policies. We wish to rule out here the use of wage and price controls on the basis that they involve too many other economic and social costs to make them a socially desirable policy tool for this purpose.

This leaves inflation as the basic macro-economic tool which, even at moderate rates, reduces real wages eventually if nominal wages fail to adjust completely. This process is likely to take a long time and we are not hopeful that organized labour in Canada will be willing to make the real-wage concessions needed to restore health to the economy. We have noted above that the interests of the unemployed minority carry very little weight in the views and decisions of the interest groups of employees. No union leaders or heads of associations of teachers, professors, lawyers or doctors can afford to face the next election on a platform of recommended real-wage reductions for their constituents to eliminate the problem of the unemployed.

For these reasons, the only but also the most basic contribution that Canadian governments can make to the solution of real-wage unemployment is to restore the competitiveness of labour markets. This means primarily the reduction of the power of unions by appropriate changes in labour codes. The codes must be made to redress the balance of power regarding certification and decertification votes, strike votes, picketing and many other aspects of the law. It also means reduction in unemployment insurance benefits and coverage. In addition, deregulation and privatization have to be expanded. Immigration policies must be oriented more towards the needs of the economy. We do not like these policies and are aware of the fact that they are incompatible with some of the most cherished values, beliefs and ideologies held by the Canadian public. Most Canadians have a great sense of justice and empathy for the unfortunate of this world. They perceive unions to be an instrument for the creation of a just society and they believe that the quality of life in Canada is enhanced by Crown corporations, regulation and fair social insurance programs. It will not come easily to them that the long-term reduction of unemployment requires some sacrifice of these goals.

However, no degree of wishful thinking will change the nature of the choice or the magnitude of the trade-off between unemployment and institutions and policies that affect the competitiveness of labour markets and through it the perceived fairness of society. They have both been neglected for too long in the public debate over unemployment, even though they have been known for as long as governments have made it their business to create a more just society. Certainly, the analysis and conclusions of this study will not disappear by labelling them ideological. Politicians of all persuasions owe it to their constituents that the problems be discussed openly and that ultimately there be an acceptance of the fact that the trade-off exists and needs to be addressed in public policies.

Some wider implications of the choice

The policy choices under discussion are relevant for more than Canada and recent years. They are also relevant for European countries, where the issue has been debated much more intensively than in North America. And it applies to the United States, where a steady growth in regulation and social insurance spending has also been accompanied by a steady upward trend in unemployment rates. Reaganomics has only slowed the growth of these programs.

The preceding policy discussion deliberately neglected Keynesian demand management. This is not to be construed as a suggestion that it is irrelevant. Neo-classical unemployment theory recognizes the existence of business cycles and the accompanying unemployment as two of the greatest problems of market economies. What is obvious from this study is, however, that the Keynesian prescriptions of easy money and large deficits did not and cannot solve the problems of the 1980s and cannot bring back the golden 1960s. A lowering of real wages and a restoration of incentives for the use of proper labour-intensive technology will restore confidence. This will encourage consumer and investment spending needed for economic growth and prosperity more reliably and effectively than easier monetary policy and larger spending deficits.

Finally, we should note that the restoration of competitive labour markets does not mean a slowdown in technological progress and productivity growth. Schumpeterian entrepreneurs continually search for new products and technologies that make them rich. Many of them succeed by introducing labour-saving technology and by lowering the prices at which they sell their products and services. As a result they expand sales and require more labour which they can obtain only by hiring from other employers and by paying higher wages. It is through this process that wages have been raised in centuries past, long before there were unions and in countries like Hong Kong and Taiwan, where unions have very little power. Labour markets dominated by powerful interest groups lead to *excessively* labour-saving technology. Only competitive labour markets assure the introduction of the *appropriate* technology.

APPENDIX

ON THE STRUCTURE OF WAGES

In this Appendix we analyze some data concerning the earnings of professors in Canada and the United States, both in relation to the average weekly earnings that were the focus of attention in the main part of the paper. The purpose of this analysis is to introduce further evidence on the lack of competitiveness in the Canadian relative to the U.S. labour market, giving special attention to the returns to a profession with high levels of human capital. We have chosen to deal with university professors because of the ready availability of data on earnings and, unfortunately, do not have any evidence about the extent to which they are representative of workers with higher skills generally. Nevertheless, we believe that the data shed some further light on the causes of the divergence of the Canadian and U.S. unemployment rates in recent years.

A 1. SOME THEORY

The theory of wage structure is relatively simple. At any given moment during their working life people's earnings reflect the time involved in acquiring their training. That is why at age 40 doctors, lawyers and professors normally earn more than do carpenters, waiters and sales-clerks. Life-time earnings are an increasing function of the danger and unpleasantness of the work. That is why forestry workers and miners tend to earn more than typists and sales clerks. Wages are higher when employment is more unstable. That is why plumbers in the private sector normally earn more than plumbers working for a government agency.

In many cases these relationships are disturbed by people earning returns due to special athletic or artistic talents, such as athletes and entertainers.

They may also be disturbed in the case of managers and professionals who have special abilities in analytical reasoning or the handling of human relations.

While economists agree broadly on the principles of the determinants of wage structures, there is little consistent evidence and agreement on the strength of these influences. The reason is basically that no one knows how to value such things as risk and discomfort. For example, how much should tree-fallers be paid for the extra risks they take in their work as compared with all other occupations? How should one value the relative boredom of having to teach the same rudiments of arithmatic encountered by elementary school teachers with the pressures encountered by university professors who have to keep up with rapidly moving new knowledge in their fields of specialization?

Further complicating the assessment of the value of the different characteristics of occupations is the relative number of people who are interested in pursuing them for reasons that are not always economic. Thus, the social values revolution among the young people in the 1960s resulted in a more rapid growth of people interested in handicrafts and arts than before or since. Yet, the greater supply of people with such skills must depress the relative wages that they earn.

Most economists conclude from the preceding that efficient and fair wage structures can only be determined by market forces. When these forces work, the premium paid to tree-fallers over other workers is the product of the joint need of the companies to find such workers and workers' ability to refuse the position unless they are satisfied that it compensates them appropriately for the risks they incur. Unfortunately, union rules, professional associations and government rules interfere with this process. Most important and relevant for this study, government employment invites workers to use political power to influence pay structures.

Because of our limited ability as economists to assess the appropriateness of occupational wage differences, the following analysis concentrates on the documentation of empirical developments and historic comparisons. We will present some presumptions, but in the end readers have to form their own views on the appropriateness of the development of the wage structures in Canada, the United States and British Columbia. Furthermore, readers should remember that the main purpose of this study is to find causes for the divergence of the Canadian and U.S. unemployment rates in recent years, not to explain the divergence of wage structures.

A 2. PROFESSORS' INCOMES IN
CANADA AND THE UNITED STATES

Figure A1 shows that between 1961 and 1972 the inflation-adjusted, real earnings of professors in Canadian universities and those of the general population increased at nearly the same rates.[12] However, thereafter professors' incomes fell for two years and a gap of about 10 percent maximum developed. The gap was closed in 1977 and in the following seven years professorial incomes fluctuated more widely than average weekly earnings, though the average growth rates were nearly the same. Only since 1982 have the professorial incomes grown consistently more rapidly than average weekly earnings, producing the largest gap in the professors' favour during the entire period under observation.

The main conclusion we may draw from Figure A1 is that professors' incomes in Canada appear to have been determined by the same forces that have determined the incomes of all other employees in the economy. As a result, between 1961 and 1983 the real incomes of the two groups under study have grown at identical rates. This is a rather remarkable fact beside which the divergence in 1983-84 seems rather insignificant. The data suggest that, unless something unusual has happened since 1981, this divergence will again be eliminated in the future, just as it has been in the past.

Canada and U.S. comparison

Figure A2 compares the real income growth of professors and average income earners in Canada and the United States. Because of a lack of data, the series starts in 1971 at 100. All of the nominal income series were deflated by the respective countries' consumer price indices to obtain the real-wage series in the graph. We remind readers again that the concern

---

12. The data presented in this Appendix are broad averages, as they are published in the sources cited in the figures. For the accurate comparison of income series of different groups of individuals, it is necessary to adjust them for differences in age, sex, training levels, regional concentration and many other influences on averages that distort their meaning for the analytical purposes at hand. We do not have the resources to make these adjustments. Therefore, readers should be aware of the limitations of the data presented here. As a matter of intuition, however, we feel that for most of the comparisons, the biases due to the omitted adjustments are not serious.

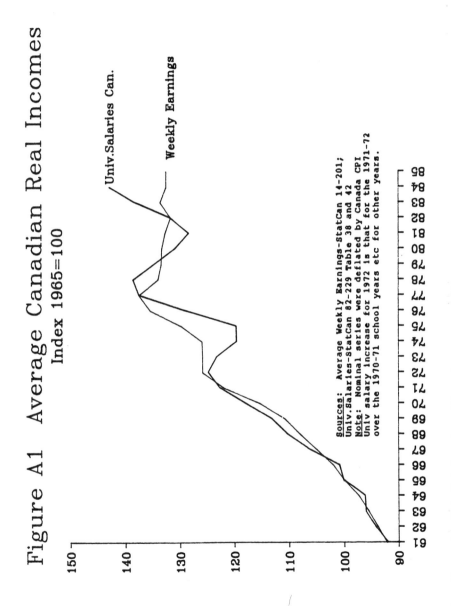

Figure A1 Average Canadian Real Incomes
Index 1965=100

Univ.Salaries Can.

Weekly Earnings

Sources: Average Weekly Earnings-StatCan 14-201;
Univ.Salaries-StatCan 82-229 Table 38 and 42
Note: Nominal series were deflated by Canada CPI
Univ salary increase for 1972 is that for the 1971-72
over the 1970-71 school years etc for other years.

Fig. A2 Av. Real Incomes Canada and USA
Index 1971=100

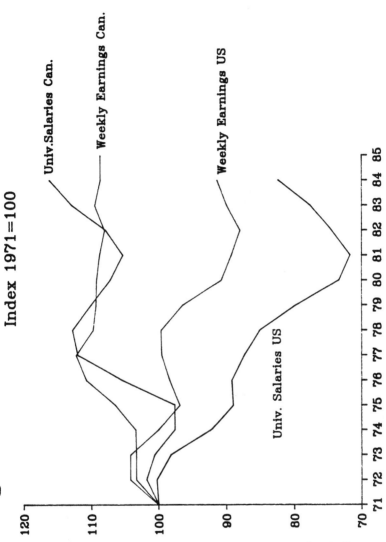

Sources: Average Weekly Earnings - Canada StatCan
14-201; USA Econ.Rep.of the President, Febr.1985
Table B 39. Univ.Salaries - Canada StatCan 82-229
Table 38 and 42; USA - Academe, Bullet. of the Amer.
Assoc. of Univ. Prof., Annual Report on the Econ.
Status of the Profession, various issues.
Note: Nominal series were deflated by the respective
country's CPI. Univ salary increase for 1972 is that
for the 1971-72 over the 1970-71 school years etc for
other years.

of this study is with trends and not levels.[13] The graph merely documents the different growth rates experienced by the income groups in the two countries.[14]

The top two lines of Figure A2 repeat the information contained in Figure A1, though the different base year exaggerates the differences in the two income series. Yet, the main conclusion remains. Between the years 1981 and 1982 the two lines crossed, indicating that during the preceding ten years in Canada average and professorial real wages rose by identical percentages.

The U.S. experience has been much different. In the main part of the study we have discussed at length the drop in U.S. real average earnings during the period and the wide gap with Canadian real earnings during this period. What is new and startling is the development of professorial average incomes. As can be seen, these incomes fell by nearly 30 percent between 1971 and 1981. The recovery during the following two years has still resulted in a drop of over 20 percent since 1971.

American professors lost not only absolutely but also relative to other income earners in the United States. In 1981 the gap reached a maximum of about 20 percentage points and it has narrowed only slightly since. The gap in real income growth between Canadian and U.S. professors' income

---

13. In the year 1981-82 the salaries of professors at U.S. colleges and universities averaged U.S. $25,750, at all Canadian universities averaged Can. $39,880 and at B.C. universities averaged $43,810. During that year the exchange rate averaged about $1.22. As a result, the U.S. dollar equivalent of the Canadian salaries was $32,688 and $35,910 for Canada and British Columbia, respectively. These figures imply a margin of 27 percent and 39 percent in favour of Canadian professors' salaries. These numbers must be interpreted with great care since the U.S. averages include colleges and the Canadian ones do not. This difference does not bias the **growth** figures used in the text as long as there has not been a significant proportion of university and college teachers in the United States and incomes of the two groups have not diverged much.

14. It is also important to remind the reader about the fact that international comparisons of incomes require that national nominal incomes be deflated either by national inflation statistics or by exchange rate changes, never both. In the main part of the study, we have compared income trends in the two countries using consumer prices in one chart and exchange rates in another. The results were nearly the same. For this reason, we limit our deflation here to the consumer price index.

has been substantial since the mid-70s and has been around 35 to 40 percentage points during the last years under observation.[15]

An interpretation

We do not know of any research that explains the poor performance of professorial incomes in the United States in the 1970s relative to that of other income groups in that country and Canada. Therefore, the following hypothesis has to be considered tentative and exploratory.

In this spirit, we postulate that U.S. professorial wage developments were dominated by first exogenous shifts in demand and subsequent dynamic processes of adjustment to excess supplies. Thus, the launching of Sputnik in the late 1950s resulted in a major U.S. government effort to expand university education levels and standards. It produced a major excess demand for professors, which raised their wages above long-run equilibrium and resulted in the immigration of many highly skilled people, the so-called brain drain, from Canada and the rest of the world to the United States.

However, during the 1970s demographic developments and lowered government support for higher education resulted in a relative decrease of demand for professors. Supplies, which were determined by the expansionary phase of the 1960s and came onto the market partly with a lag, generated conditions of excess supplies. Under the pressure of these excess supplies, the incomes of professors declined in the manner evident from Figure A2.

Since the Canadian and U.S. markets for professors are highly integrated, the postulated excess demand during the 1960s in the United States should have produced a similar disequilibrium and subsequent need for readjustment in Canada. Figure A1 suggests that this has not been the case. The main explanation for this development may well lie in differences in the labour markets of the two countries which we discussed in the main part of the paper.

It is recalled that in the main part of this study we advanced as the main explanation of the divergence of average weekly earnings of workers in Canada and the United States the different levels of unionization and unemployment insurance spending in the two countries. A similar set of

---

15. These results may go a long way towards explaining why the concern with the brain drain from Canada in the 1960s was replaced largely in the 1970s and 1980s by a concern over how to keep Canadian academic positions reserved for Canadians.

explanations is also consistent with the different rates of professorial income growth in the two countries.

In the case of professors it is not unionization but the public ownership of universities which are responsible for the higher growth rate of professorial incomes in Canada. It is well known that universities in Canada are almost totally financed by governments while in the United States the role of governments is very much smaller. Moreover, in Canada the federal government has an important, if indirect role, in the financing of universities while in the United States, state governments are almost completely in control of public university financing.

As a result of these differences, there are much higher returns to political activities of university professors in support of increased public university financing in Canada than in the United States. The facts shown in Figure A2 are consistent with stronger and more effective political interest group pressures of Canadian as compared with U.S. university professors since 1971. In other words, in Canada professors' incomes have been determined relatively much more by politics than market conditions as compared to the United States.

A 3. BRITISH COLUMBIA CONDITIONS

Figure A3 shows the growth of income of university teachers in Canada and the province of British Columbia. We introduce these data here because we believe that they shed further light on the causes of the divergence of real incomes of different groups of people in the economy. Therefore, they strengthen the findings in the main part of the paper that labour market organization strongly influences wage levels and, therefore, real-wage unemployment.

It can be seen from the time-series that from 1972 to 1982-83 the cumulative growth rate of professorial salaries in B.C. was about 7 percentage points above that in all of Canada. This gap was created to a very large extent between 1972 and 1975. During this period British Columbia was governed by the New Democratic Party (NDP). This party's election platform is dominated by a socialist approach to economic management. Some of its main and most loyal groups of political supporters have been and are university professors. The relative wage gains of B.C. professors during these years are at least consistent with the hypothesis that they are a form of political reward or, put differently, the returns to, political activism of a special interest group.

The more market-oriented Socred government which has been in power

Fig. A3   Average University Salaries
Index 1971=100

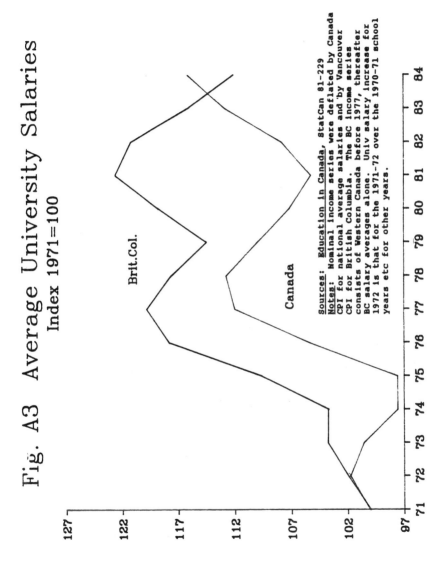

Brit.Col.

Canada

Sources: Education in Canada, StatCan 81-229
Notes: Nominal income series were deflated by Canada
CPI for national average salaries and by Vancouver
CPI for British Columbia. The BC income series
consists of Western Canada before 1977, thereafter
BC salary averages alone. Univ salary increase for
1972 is that for the 1971-72 over the 1970-71 school
years etc for other years.

in British Columbia since 1975 encountered a severe financial crisis in 1981 and initiated an austerity program. It curtailed sharply the growth of university budgets and as a result the real salaries of professors dropped by nearly 10 percent, just when those in the rest of Canada began to rise. By 1984 parity of B.C. and all of Canada professorial salaries was restored. The political cost of fighting some of the austerity battle on the backs of universities, of course, has probably been considered to be rather slim for the governing Socred party since professors' loyalties are with the NDP anyway. Strong and known interest group loyalties to specific parties have their benefits as well as their disadvantages.

A 4. SUMMARY AND SOME IDEAS ON POLICY

In this Appendix we have assembled data on the growth in relative real incomes of professors in Canada and the United States. The much greater income growth of Canadian university professors was hypothesized to have been due to the more prominent role of governments as the employers of professors in Canada as compared to the United States. As a result, there is less competition and more returns to political lobbying in the Canadian than the U.S. market for professors. The importance of interest group politics was also found evident in the historic development of the relative incomes of B.C. university professors compared with those in the rest of Canada.

We interpret the evidence on the divergence of the relative salaries as being in further support of the thesis that wage flexibility generally in Canada is less than in the United States because of differences in the level of unionization, the strength of unions and the importance of government as an employer. Because of these differences in recent years Canada has suffered much more than the United States from real-wage unemployment.

A policy proposal

The preceding analysis suggests the desirability of removing the setting of wages of professors from the political process. In principle, this could be done by the privatization of the existing universities. Under such an institutional approach, the government could continue to meet its obligations towards the subsidy of higher education by providing students with vouchers redeemable at the university chosen by the students. Research in the public interest could be financed by project and institutional grants.

However, it is highly unlikely that the preceding proposals will ever be adopted in British Columbia because of the opposition from organized lobby groups of professors and teachers. They would argue that the efficiency benefits of privatization are not proved and that public ownership of educational facilities is an essential part of a humanitarian society which assures the greatest possible fairness and equality of opportunity for all. The general population and voters would probably support these arguments. Professors and teachers, of course, would be reluctant to discuss the fact that they also like very much the civil service status and absence from competitive pressures that accompanies public ownership of educational institutions.

Under the assumption that the first best solution through privatization is not attainable, we propose the following second best institutional procedures for the determination of professors' salaries.[16] The government maintains current statistics of pay levels in the private sector, differentiating between the pay of secretaries, junior executives and similar classes of employees characterized by different levels of training, risk and discomfort. Professorial salaries are then linked to those in the private sector by a formula. For example, professorial salaries would be made equal to x percent of the salaries of junior executives.

Under this system parliament and the political process have to face squarely the issue whether x should be 80, 90 or 110 percent. Professors can make representation about the merit of different numbers. They can be expected to argue about efficiency, the long-run quality of education and fairness. Political parties could write into their election platforms what numbers they support. The democratic process would thus be likely to result in professorial salaries that represent a social consensus on the relative importance of efficiency, equity and quality.

The proposed system would be vastly more desirable than the present one, which has resulted in the excessively large increases during the reign of the NDP and the harsh adjustment in later years when the slowdown in the growth of tax receipts forced cutbacks. These cutbacks were based on the argument that the lower tax receipts required a cut-back of all government services. This argument was opposed on the grounds that tax increases or temporary deficit financing should be used to assure the stability of the educational system.

---

16. The proposal would obviously be applicable also to the determination of the wages of other public employees such as teachers and welfare workers. For a more detailed analysis of the issues surrounding public service employee compensation see Christensen (1980).

There is no objective counter-argument against this kind of reasoning. As a result, the government has emphasized repeatedly that the decrease in professorial salaries was necessary also on the grounds that private sector wages had failed to rise and that, therefore, professorial salaries were getting out of line with historic relationships. As the preceding analysis suggests, this emphasis on private sector relationships is appropriate. Our proposal merely involves the formalization of a wage-setting principle for public sector employees that appears to be in effect informally, and that generates unnecessary political adversity and costs to the political party in power.

There are no perfect solutions to the problem of how professors' salaries and public sector wages generally should be determined. But given the magnitude of the problem, the proposal presented here should deserve at least closer scrutiny.

References

Bossons, J. and D.P. Dungan, "The Government Deficit: Too High or Too Low?," *Can. Tax J.*, Jan.-Febr. 1983.

Christensen, Sandra, *Unions and the Public Interest*, Vancouver, The Fraser Institute, 1980.

Daly, D.J., "Cost Competitiveness in Canadian Manufacturing: The Challenge and Some Policy Options," York University, Processed October, 1984.

_____, "Canada's International Competitive Position," a paper prepared for the National Economic Conference, March 1985, in Ottawa.

Giersch, H. and F. Wolter, "Towards an Explanation of the Productivity Slowdown: An Acceleration-Deceleration Hypothesis," *Econ. J.*, 93, March 1983.

Gordon, R.J., "An Outsider's View of the British Debate on Wages and Unemployment," Northwestern University and Centre for Economic Policy Research, Processed, March 1985.

Grubb, D. et al., "Wage Rigidity and Unemployment in OECD Countries," *Europ. Econ. Rev.*, 21, 1983.

Grubel, H.G., "Canadian Monetary Policy as a Reflection of Major Trends in Economic Theory 1959-81," *West. Econ. Rev.*, 1983.

Grubel, H.G. and M. Walker, editors, *Unemployment Insurance: Global Evidence of Its Effects on Unemployment*, Vancouver: The Fraser Institute, 1978.

Grubel, H.G. and Z. Spindler, "Bonus Pay Systems for Greater Economic Stability," *Can. Pub. Policy*, June 1984.

Gylfason, T. and A. Lindbeck, "Union Rivalry and Wages: An Oligopolistic Approach," *Economica*, forthcoming.

Hamermesh, D.S., "The Demand for Labour in the Long Run," in O. Ashenfelter and R. Layard, eds., *Handbook of Labour Economics*, Amsterdam: North Holland, (forthcoming).

Helliwell, J., "Recent Evidence from Macroeconomic Models of the Canadian Economy," in *Macroeconomics: Theory, Policy and Evidence*, Inst. of Social and Econ. Res., Univ. of Manitoba, 1983.

_____, "Stagflation and Productivity Decline in Canada 1974-82," *Can. J. Econ.*, 1984.

H.M. Treasury, "The Relationship Between Employment and Wages," London, Jan. 1985.

Kaliski, S.F., "Why Must Unemployment Remain so High?," *Can. Pub. Policy*, X,2, June 1984, pp. 127-41.

Lindbeck, A. and D.J. Snower, "Explanations of Unemployment," *Oxford Rev. Econ. Policy*, 1,2, 1985.

MacDonald, G.M., "The Size and Structure of Union-Nonunion Wage Differentials in Canadian Industry," *Can. J. Econ.*, Aug. 1983.

Malinvaud, E., "Wages and Unemployment," *Econ. J.*, 1982.

McCallum, J. "Unemployment in OECD Countries in the 1980s: Keynesian or Classical?, Univ. of Quebec in Montreal, Mimeo. Disc. Paper, April 1984.

_____, "Wage Gaps, Factor Shares and Real Wages," forthcoming, *Scandin. J. Econ.*

McDonald, I. and R.M. Solow, "Wage Bargaining and Employment," *Am. Econ. Rev.*, 71, 1981.

Mincer, J., "Unemployment Effects of Minimum Wages," *J.P.E.* 1976.

Mone, L., "The $52 Billion Surplus: What Washington Can Learn from States and Cities," *Policy Review*, Spring 1985.

OECD, *Employment Outloook*, Paris, Sept. 1985.

Riddell, C.W. and P.M. Smith, "Expected Inflation and Wage Changes in Canada 1967-81," *Can. J. Econ.*, Aug. 1982.

Stigler, G., "The Theory of Economic Regulation," *Bell J. of Econ.*, Spring 1971.

West, E.G. and M. McKee, *Minimum Wages: The New Issues in Theory, Evidence, Policy and Politics*, Ottawa: Economic Council of Canada and The Institute for Research on Public Policy, 1980.